PRAYER BOOK

by
Anna Riva

Author of:
Power of the Psalms
Candle Burning Magic
Devotion to the Saints
Secret of Magical Seals
Modern Herbal Spell book
Modern Witchcraft Spell book
Golden Secrets of Mystic Oils
Spellcraft, Hexcraft & Witchcraft
Voodoo Handbook of Cult Secrets
Your Lucky Number...Forever
How to Conduct a Séance

INDIO PRODUCTS
www.indioproducts.com

Copyright© 1984
Reprint 2009

Occult Books • Curios • Supplies

ISBN 0-9438-3209-8

NOTICE: All rights reserved. No part of this book may be reproduced in any form without prior written permission of the publisher. No claims of supernatural effects or powers are made for any item mentioned herein, and the material is strictly legendary.

INTRODUCTION

Within these pages, the reader will find selections of prose and poetry selected from over 2,500 years of inspirational literature. Over two hundred authors are represented, ranging from Archiloches, the Greek poet who lived from about 700 to 650 BC, and Aristophanes, a comic poet of Athens who was born about 448 BC and produced plays which mixed political, social, and literary satire...on through the writers of the almost two thousand years since the birth of Christ, including Shakespeare, Omar Khayyam, Dickens, Goldsmith, Whittier, Donne, the Brontes, Dickinson, Ruskin, Stevenson, and a few personal prayers and snippets of verse by the author, plus a variety of message from those unsung anonymous writers.

The book is arranged by subject so that one can turn easily to the section of immediate need. Each selection bears a numerical number opposite its first line or title on the right hand side. This number corresponds to the author index which is in alphabetical order at the end of the book. The author index gives the entire page numbers on which that writer's work appears.

To illustrate, if you wish to read about Patience, in the Subject Index you will find that it is on Page 5. Turn to that page and find all the entries which may help, inspire, or give you insight into varying points of view on this subject. Should a particular entry appeal, you may want to see what that author had to say about other matters so check the number on the right beside the entry, and turn to the Author Index. Skim down the numerical list and match the number of the entry with its author. Beside that name, you will find to the right all of the page numbers on which some of his or her work is given.

It is my hope that this book will provide many hours of solace, guidance, inspiration, and joy. Should you have some favorite pieces of writings which you would like to see included in such a collection, you are invited to send them to the author for consideration in a future edition.

I leave you with this piece by an unknown writer which sums up an ideal philosophy for a joyous life.

> Give strength, give thought, give deed, and give wealth;
> Give love, give tears and give thyself.
> Give, give, and be always giving,
> Who gives not is not living;
> The move you give, the more you live.

ANNA RIVA
Spring,1984

Today
is the
First Day
of the
Rest of your
Life

SUBJECT INDEX

TODAY!

With every rising of the sun
Think of your life as just begun.

The Past has concealed and buried deep
All yesterdays. There let them sleep.

Concern yourself with but Today.
Grasp it, and teach it to obey

Your will and plan. Since time began
Today has been the friend of man.

You and Today! A soul sublime
and the great heritage of time.

With God Himself to bind the twain,
Go forth, brave heart! Attain! Attain!

ABOUT PRAYER

****

Prayer, that approach to the deity in words or thoughts, can provide solace, comfort, guidance, answers, and bring calm peace to the supplicant. Pray sincerely, pray often, and pray thoughtfully for you may get what you pray for! And, once your plea has been sent on its way, quiet yourself and listen for the answer for it will surely come.

****

PRAYER 41

Be not afraid to pray—to pray is right
Pray, if thou canst, with hope; but ever pray,
Though hope is weak, or sick with long delay;
Pray in the darkness, if there be no light,
Far is the time, remote from human sight,
When war and discord on the earth shall cease,
Yet every prayer for universal peace
Avails the blessed time to expedite.

Whate'er is good to wish, ask that of Heaven,
Though it is what thou canst not hope to see:
Pray to be perfect, though material leaven
Forbid the spirit so on earth to be;
But if for any wish thou darest not pray,
Then pray to God to cast that wish away.

A prayer in its simplest definition is merely a wish turned Godward 24

It is good for us to keep some account of our prayers, that we may not unsay them in our practice. 96

Every time you pray, if your prayer is sincere, there will be a new feeling and new meaning in it which gives you fresh courage, and you will understand that prayer is an education. 55

Call on God, but row away from the rocks. 170-D

To serve God is not to pass our lives on our knees in prayer; it is to discharge on earth those obligations which our duty requires. 179

All who call on God in true faith, earnestly from the heart, will certainly be heard, and will receive what they have asked and desired, although not in the hour or in the measure, or the very thing which they ask; yet they will obtain something greater and more glorious than they had dared to ask. 137

I have been driven many times to my knees by the overwhelming conviction that I had nowhere else to go. My own wisdom and that of all about me seemed insufficient for the day. 130

God is better served in resisting a temptation to evil than in many formal prayers. 167

ABOUT PRAYER

It is not well for a man to pray cream and live skim milk. 16

How marvelous that I, a filthy clod, 183
May yet hold friendly converse with my God!

Do not pray for easy lives; pray to be stronger men. 24
Do not pray for tasks equal to your powers pray for power equal to your tasks.

Like one who leaves the trampled street 198
For some cathedral, cool and dim,
Where he can hear in music beat
The heart of prayer, that beats for him;
Restored and comforted, I go
To grapple with my tasks again;
Through silent worship taught to know
The blessed peace that follows pain.

Lord, I know not what I ought to ask of Thee; Thou only knowest 69
what I need; Thou lovest me better than I know how to love myself. O Father, give to Thy child that which he himself knows not how to ask. I present myself before Thee, I open my heart to Thee. Behold my needs which I know not myself; see and do according to Thy tender mercy. I offer myself in sacrifice. I yield myself to Thee, I would have no other desire than to accomplish Thy will. Teach me to pray. Pray Thyself in me.

For me, prayer is an uplifting of the heart, a glance toward Heaven, a 181-T-2
cry of gratitude and of love in times of sorrow as well as of joy. It is sometimes noble, something supernatural, which expands the soul and unites it to God.

More things are wrought by prayer 200
Than this world dreams of.
Wherefore, let thy voice
Rise like a fountain for me night and day.
For what are men better than sheep or goats
That nourish a blind life within the brain,
If, knowing God, they lift not hands of prayer
Both for themselves and those who call them friends?
For so the whole round earth is every way
Bound by gold chains about the feet of God.

What I have learned is this: that the entire foundation of prayer must 181-T-1
be established in humility, and that, the more a soul abases itself in prayer, the higher God raises it.

Prayer should be the key of the day and the lock of the night. 97

ABOUT PRAYER

When you say your prayers, you must go into your private room, and shut the door, and say your prayers to your Father who is in secret. And your Father, who sees what is done in secret, will give you your reward in full. For, when the door is shut, someone prays in his private room when, while his mouth is silent, he pours forth the affection of his heart in the sight of the heavenly pity. And the voice is heard in secret, when it cries out in silence with the holy desires. 181-G-2

Meditation teaches us what it is that we lack, and prayer obtains it. Meditation shows us the way, and prayer makes us walk therein. Finally, meditation lets us know the dangers which threaten us, and prayer makes us avoid them by the grace of Our Lord Jesus Christ. 181-B-4

Prayer is and remains the native and deepest impulse of the soul of man. 36

Spiritual joy arises from purity of the heart and perseverance in prayer. 181-F-2

PRAYER 153

Prayer is the soul's sincere desire.
Uttered or unexpressed;
The motion of a hidden fire,
That trembles in the breast.

Prayer is the burden of a sigh;
The falling of a tear;
The upward glancing of an eye,
When none but God is near.

Prayer is the simplest form of speech
That infant lips can try;
Prayer, the sublimest strains that reach
The Majesty on high.

When thou prayest, rather let thy heart be without words than thy words without heart. 30

A strict belief in fate is the worst kind of slavery; on the other hand there is comfort in the thought that God will be moved by our prayers. 65

He prays well who is so absorbed with God that he does not know he is praying. 181-F-1

Prayer does not change God, but changes him who prays. 121

ACCEPTANCE

****

There is no growth of character when blessings are falling on our lives, but true worth is increased when hardship and tragedy is borne with quiet composure and tranquility.

****

To struggle when hope is banished! 116
To live when life's salt is gone!
To dwell in a dream that's vanished—
To endure, and go calmly on!

That is best which God sends; it was his will; it is mine. 150

O Lord, if only my will may remain right and firm towards Thee, 118
do with me whatsoever it shall please Thee. For it cannot be anything but good, whatsoever Thou shalt do with me. If it be Thy will I should be in darkness, be Thou blessed; and, if it be Thy will I should be in light, be Thou again blessed. If thou vouchsafe to comfort me, be Thou blessed; and, if Thou wilt have me afflicted, be Thou equally blessed. O Lord! For Thy sake I will cheerfully suffer whatever shall come on me with Thy permission.

Be willing to have it so. Acceptance of what has happened is the first 112
step to overcoming the consequences of any misfortune.

And yet these days of dreariness are sent us from above; 8
They do not come in anger, but in faithfulness and love;
They come to teach us lessons which bright ones could not yield,
And to leave us blest and thankful when their purpose is fulfilled.

As Thou wilt, O Lord, 118
Thou knowest what is best for us;
Let this or that be done, as Thou shalt please.
Give what Thou wilt, and how much Thou wilt,
and when Thou wilt.
Deal with me as Thou thinkest good.
Set me where Thou wilt, and deal with me in all
things just as Thou wilt.
Behold, I am Thy servant, prepared for all things:
For I desire not to live unto myself, but unto Thee:
And oh, that I could do it worthily and perfectly!

However mean your life is, meet it and live it; do not shun it and call 201
it hard names. It is not so bad as you are. It looks poorest when you are richest. The fault-finder will find faults even in Paradise. Love your life, poor as it is. You may perhaps have some pleasant, thrilling, glorious hours, even in a poorhouse.

Yet I argue not against Heav'n's hand or will, 152
nor bate one jot of heart or hope,
but still bear up and steer right onward.

ADVERSITY

****

Our strengths are never really known until we are met with ill-fortune or hard times. It is in our troubled times that we gain whatever energy and stamina necessary to meet our needs.

****

Adversity has the effect of eliciting talents which, in prosperous 102
circumstances, would have lain dormant.

Sweet are the uses of adversity; 186
Which, like the toad, ugly and venomous,
Wears yet a precious jewel in his head.

When God shuts a door, He opens a window. 180

It is by those who have suffered that the world has been advanced 202

Misfortune is never mournful to the soul that accepts it; for such do 181-J-1
always see that in every cloud is an angel's face.

There is nothing the body suffers that the soul may not profit by. 149

When you get into a tight place and everything goes against you, till it 196
seems as though you could not hold on a minute longer, never give up
then, for that is just the place and time that the tide will turn.

Most merciful God, allow this pain I bear to serve as a reminder of the 175
greater suffering you have borne. Enfold me with thy love for I know
the hurt will subside in time, but your light will shine on me always.
Mercifully accept this prayer, and grant thy servant the help of thy
power.

Lord, we pray not for tranquility, nor that our tribulations may cease; 182
we pray for Thy spirit and Thy love, that Thou grant us strength and
grace to overcome adversity.

Affliction comes to us all not to make us sad; but sober, not to make us 16
sorry, but wise; not to make us despondent, but by its darkness to
refresh us, as the night refreshes the day; not to impoverish, but to
enrich us, as the plough enriches the field; to multiply our joy, as the
seed, by planting, is multiplied a thousand-fold.

BENEDICTIONS

****

A short prayer completes a meal, concludes a meeting, or blesses a parting with dignity and with love.

****

I pray the prayer many others do 8
May the peace of God abide with you,
Wherever you stay, wherever you go,
May the mighty love of God also grow,
Through days of labor and nights of rest,
The love of God will make you blest.

Guide us through life; and when at last we enter into rest, 138
Thy tender arms around us cast, and fold us to Thy breast.

Lord, dismiss us with Thy blessing 90
Hope and comfort from above;
Let us each, Thy peace possessing,
Triumph in redeeming love.

The Lord bless thee, and keep thee; 20-A
The Lord make his face shine upon thee, and be gracious unto thee;
The Lord lifts up his countenance upon thee, and give thee peace.

The grace of the Lord Jesus Christ, and the love of God, and the communion of the Holy Ghost, be with you all. 20-A

May the road rise up to meet you 170-E
May the wind be always at your back,
May the sun shine warm upon your face,
And the rain fall soft upon your fields,
And until we meet again,
May God hold you in the palm of His hand.

PEACE BE WITH YOU 8
I pray the prayer the Easterners do,
May the peace of Allah abide with you;
Wherever you stay, wherever you go,
May the beautiful palms of Allah grow;
Through days of labor and nights of rest,
The love of good Allah make you blest.

The grace of God the Father and the peace of our Lord Jesus Christ, through the fellowship of the Holy Spirit, dwell with us forever. 34

The Lord watch between me and thee, when we are absent one from another. 20-A

BLESSINGS

****

Blessings—those gifts from God which seem to come to us in almost direct proportion to our faith and gratitude.

****

Reflect upon your present blessings, of which every man has many, 51
not on your past misfortunes, of which all men have some.

Thrist blest whose lives are faithful prayers, 200
Whose loves in higher love endure;
What souls possess themselves so pure,
Or is there blessedness like theirs?

May the blessing of God await thee. May the sun of glory shine around 51
thy bed; and may the gates of plenty, honor, and happiness be ever open to thee. May no sorrow distress thy days; may no grief disturb thy nights. May the pillow of peace kiss thy cheek, and the pleasures of imagination attend thy dreams; and when length of years make thee tired of earthly joys, and the curtain of death gently closes around thy last sleep of human existence, may the Angel of God attend thy bed, and take care that the expiring lamp of life shall not receive one rude blast of hasten on its extinction.

How silently, how silently, 24
The wondrous gift is given;
So God imparts to human hearts
The blessings of His heaven.
No ear may hear His coming;
But in the world of sin
Where meek souls will receive Him still
The dear Christ enters in.

All blessings come to us through our Lord. He will teach us, for in 181-T-1
beholding his life we find that he is our best example. What more do we desire from such a good friend at our side? Unlike our friends in the world, he will never abandon us when we are troubled or distressed. Blessed is the one who truly loves him and always keeps him near.

How blessings brighten as they take their flight! 217

May the King eternal, immortal, invisible, the only wise God, bless and 20-A
protect us, this day and forever.

Give me thy blessings as I face the tasks of life. Show me the way 175
toward all that is good, and warn me when I stray from the path you would have me trod. Guide my feet toward your kingdom, place in my hands the work you would have them do, and instill in my mouth only those words which are kind toward those to whom and of whom I speak. Keep my mind clear and clean with thoughts which are acceptable and pleasing to you.

CHILDREN'S PRAYERS

****

In Mark 10:14, it is written, "Suffer the little children to come unto me, and forbid them not; for of such is the kingdom of God."

****

BEFORE SLEEPING 8

Matthew, Mark, Luke and John,
Bless the bed that I lie on.
Before I lay me down to sleep,
I give my soul to Christ to keep.
Four corners to my bed,
Four angels there spread,
Two to foot and two to head,
And four to carry me when I'm dead.
I go by sea, I go by land,
The Lord made me with His right hand.
If any danger come to me,
Sweet Jesus Christ, deliver me.
He's the branch and I'm the flower,
Pray God send me a happy hour,
And if I die before I wake,
I pray that Christ my soul will take.

A CHILD'S GRACE 8

God is great and God is good,
And we thank him for our food.
By His hand we all are fed,
Give us, Lord, our daily bread.

NOW I LAY ME DOWN TO SLEEP 8

Now I lay me down to sleep.
I pray Thee, Lord, Thy child to keep;
Thy loves go with me all the night
And wake me with the morning light.

GENTLE JESUS, MEEK AND MILD 8

Gentle Jesus, meek and mild,
Look upon a little child;
Pity my simplicity,
Suffer me to come to Thee.

Fain I would to Thee be brought;
Gracious God, forbid it not:
In the kingdom of Thy grace
Give a little child a place.

Oh, supply my every want,
Feed the young and tender plant;
Day and night my keeper be,
Every moment watch o'er me.

CHILDREN'S PRAYERS

Little things 8
On little wings
Bear little souls to heaven

GRACE 98

What God gives, and what we take,
'Tis a gift for Christ His sake:
Be the meal of beans and peas,
God be thanked for those, and these:
Have we flesh, or have we fish,
All are fragments from His dish. Amen

LOVING JESUS 209

Loving Jesus, meek and mild,
Look upon a little child!
Make me gentle as Thou art,
Come and live within my heart.
Take my childish hand in Thine,
Guide these little feet of mine.
So shall all my happy days
Sing their pleasant song of praise;
And the world shall always see
Christ, the Holy Child, in me.

GOD BE IN MY HEAD 8

God be in my head
And in my understanding.
God be in mine eyes
And in my lookings.
God be in my mouth
And in my speaking.
God be in my heart
And in my thinking.
God be at mine end
And in my departing.

GOOD NIGHT 106

Good night! Good night! Far flies the light;
But still God's love shall flame above,
Making all bright. Good night! Good night!

Thank You for the world so sweet 8
Thank You for the food we eat,
Thank You for the birds that sing,
Thank You, God, for everything.

A LITTLE CHILD'S PRAYER 197

Make me, dear Lord, polite and kind
To everyone, I pray;
And may I ask you how to find
Yourself, dear Lord, today?

COURAGE

****

Almost 2,000 years ago, Plutarch wrote, "Courage consists not in hazarding without fear, but being resolutely minded in a just cause."

****

It matters not how straight the gate, 95
How charged with punishments the scroll,
I am the master of my fate:
I am the captain of my soul.

Wait on the Lord: be of good courage, and He shall strengthen thine heart: wait, I say on the Lord. 20-A

My Lord, wise men ne'er sit and wail their woes, 186
But presently prevent the ways to wail.
To fear the foe, since fear oppressed strength,
Gives in your weakness strength unto your foe,
And so your follies fight against yourself.
Fear, and be slain: no worse can come to flight.

I beg you to take courage; the brave soul can mend even disaster. 38

Courage consists not in blindly overlooking danger, but in seeing it and conquering it. 174

Wealth lost, something lost; 81
Honor lost, much lost;
Courage lost, all lost.

Courage, brother, do not stumble 140
Though thy path be dark as night;
There's a star to guide the humble;
Trust in God and do the right.

To a brave man, good and bad luck are like his right and left hand. He uses both. 181-C-1

O holy Christ, O Lord of Light, 8
Succor me now in my affright.
O holy Christ, now in this hour
Keep tryst with me and be my Tower.

He who loses wealth loses much. 39
He who loses a friend loses more.
But he that loses his courage loses all.

Have courage for the great sorrows of life and patience for the small ones; and when you have laboriously accomplished your daily task, go to sleep in peace. God is awake. 106

COURAGE

The journey of a thousand miles begins with one step. 125

Let my soul beneath her load 174
Faint not through the o'erwearied flesh;
Let me hourly drink afresh
Love and peace from Thee, my God.

Stay with me God. 8
The night is dark,
The night is cold:
My little spark of courage dies.
The night is long:
Be with me, God, and make me strong.

Difficulties are the things that show what men are. 64

Almighty God, Who knowest us to be set in the midst of so many and great dangers, that by reason of the frailty of our nature we cannot always stand upright: Grant us such strength and protection, as may support us in all dangers, and carry us through all temptations; through Jesus Christ, Thy Son, our Lord. 137

Lord, I am no hero. 122
I have been careless, cowardly, and sometimes all but mutinous.
Punishment I have deserved. I deny it not.
But a traitor I have never been; a deserter I have never been.
I have tried to fight on Thy side in Thy battle against evil.
I have tried to do the duty which lay nearest me;
and to leave whatever Thou didst commit to my charge a little
better than I found it.
I have not been good, but I have at least tried to be good.
Take the will for the deed, good Lord.
Strike not my unworthy name off the roll-call of the noble and
victorious army, which is the blessed company of all faithful people;
and let me, too, be found written in the Book of Life;
even though I stand the lowest and last upon its list.

God, give me the courage to face a fact, though it slays me. 108

If we would force ourselves to stand in battle as mighty men we should see verily the help of our Lord come from heaven: for he is ready to help all them that fight for him and trust in his grace, and suffereth us to have occasions of fighting that we may have the victory. 118

Courage, the footstool of the Virtues, upon which they stand 195

If all men were just, there would be no need of courage 168

DAILY HELP

****

If we are ever in doubt about a course of action, it is a good guide to ask ourselves what we shall wish tomorrow that we had done.

****

SUNDAY 175

Blessed is this day which has been given. Blessed is the earth, the heavens and the seas. Blessed are light and darkness, day and night, birds, beasts, and me. Let me use this day well. Let me not wander from thy commandments.

MONDAY 175

Guide me this day to keep my heart clean, my hands pure, and my mind directed toward the glory of God. Keep my tongue quiet of lies and deceit, and many blessings upon me will surely follow.

TUESDAY 175

Deal kindly, Lord, with me who lifts up mine eyes to thee. Have mercy on my weaknesses, and grant that my strength will be increased sufficient to the demands made upon me this day. For I know my help is in Thee, who made heaven and earth.

WEDNESDAY 175

Restore to me the joy of salvation. Strengthen me with a generous spirit. Create a clean heart for me. Renew in me a steadfast spirit. Deliver me from my guilt, and cleanse me from my sins. I know that light shines for the just, and joy for the upright of heart.

THURSDAY 175

Hear my prayer for my heart is faint. Restore me when my faith falters. My foolishness and my faults are known to you. Rescue me from those who hate me. With Thee is the fountain of life, and in Thy light we see light.

FRIDAY 175

Help me this day to love those who care for me, be kind to those who wish me harm, and to keep my voice gentle, my mind open, and my heart filled with the knowledge that there are many blessings for those who trust in God and keep his commandments.

SATURDAY 175

Blessed be God who is my shield and my refuge, my fortress and my deliverer. I know that the Lord renders justice to all the oppressed, forgives my faults, and heals all infirmities.

JUST FOR TODAY 212

Lord, for tomorrow and its needs
I do not pray:
Keep me, my God, from stain of sin
Just for today.
Let me both diligently work
And duly pray.
Let me be kind in word and deed
Just for Today.
Let me be slow to do my will,
Prompt to obey.
Help me to mortify my flesh
Just for today.
Let me no wrong or idle word
Unthinking say.
Set Thou a seal upon my lips
Just for today.
Let me in season, Lord, be grave,
In season gay.
Let me be faithful to Thy grace.
Just for today.
And if today my tide of life
Should ebb away
Give me Thy sacraments divine.
Sweet Lord, today.
So for tomorrow and its needs
I do not pray:
But keep me, guide me, love me, Lord;
Just for today.

And let us not clutter up today with the leavings of other days 100

His daily prayer, far better understood 211
In acts than words, was simply doing good.

For each new morning with its light, 63
Father, we thank Thee,
For rest and shelter of the night,
Father, we thank Thee,
For health and food, for love and friends,
For everything Thy goodness sends,
Father, in heaven, we thank Thee.

Do not look forward to what may happen tomorrow; the same ever-lasting Father who cares for you today will take care of you tomorrow, and every day. 181-F-1

Actions are ours; their consequences belong to heaven. 72

DAILY HELP

TODAY 36

So here hath been dawning
Another blue day.
Think, wilt thou let it
Slip useless away?

Out of eternity
This new day is born;
Into eternity,
At night, will return.

Behold it aforetime
No eye ever did;
So soon it forever
From all eyes is hid.

Here hath been dawning
Another blue day;
Think, wilt thou let it
Slip useless away?

MORNING PRAYER 195

The day returns and brings us the petty round of irritating concern and duties. Help us to play the man, help us to perform them with laughter and kind faces, let cheerfulness abound with industry. Give us to go blithely on our business all this day, bring us to our resting beds weary and content and undishonored, and grant us in the end the gift of sleep.

MORNING PRAYER 175

I come to this new day with a realization that I can make of it a time of growth. Lead me, guide me, and strengthen me as the day unfolds. Help me to see opportunities for good so that my every act and deed will be of benefit to all. Shield me with your protection as I go about my tasks with faith in Thy safe-keeping.

NOONDAY PRAYER 175

Blessed Savior, I pause at midday to thank Thee for the protection and guidance bestowed upon me during the morning hours. Shield me from temptations through the afternoon and evening time. Be at my side this day and evermore.

FOR DAILY BLESSINGS 175

Grant me clarity of mind, a healthy body, and a peaceful soul so that I may go about my daily work with composure, tranquility, and efficiency. Keep me this day in Thy eye for in Thee I put my trust.

O live in us this day, 159
O clothe thyself, thy purpose yet again
In human clay;
Work through our feebleness thy strength,
Work through our meanness thy nobility,
Work through our helpless poverty of soul
Thy grace, thy glory and thy love.

To have, each day, the thing I wish 19
Lord, that seems best to me;
But not to have the thing I wish,
Lord, that seems best to Thee.
Most truly, then, Thy will be done,
When mine, O Lord, is crossed;
'Tis good to see my plans o'erthrown,
My ways in Thine all lost.

What Thou shalt today provide, 158
Let me as a child receive;
What tomorrow may betide,
Calmly to Thy wisdom leave.
'Tis enough that Thou wilt care;
Why should I the burden bear.

Politeness is like an air cushion: there may be nothing in it, but it eases our jolts wonderfully. 115

Do all the good you can, 210
By all the means you can,
In all the ways you can,
In all the places you can,
At all the times you can,
To all the people you can,
As long as ever you can.

And what doth the Lord require of thee, but to do justly, and to love mercy, and to walk humbly with thy God? 20-A

He walked by faith and not by sight, 211
By love and not by law;
The presence of the wrong or right
He rather felt than saw.

Quiet, Lord, my forward heart 158
Make me teachable and mild,
Upright, simple, free from art,
Make me as a weaned child;
From distrust and envy free,
Pleased with all that pleaseth Thee.

DAILY HELP

NEVER MIND 8

Never mind yesterday, life is today!
Never mind yesterday, lay it away!
Never mind anything over and done,
Here is a new moment, lit with new sun.

Never mind that which was once on a time,
Tomorrow rings in with its new sheaf of rhyme.
Yesterday's shadow scarce drags down the lane
Ere silver-shod morning comes dancing again.

LOVE THE BEAUTIFUL 148

Love the beautiful
Seek out the true,
Wish for the good,
And the best do.

The happiness of your life, and its power, and its part and rank in earth 180
or in heaven, depends on the way you pass your days now. They are not to be sad days; far from that, the first duty of young people is to be delighted and delightful; but they are to be in the deepest sense solemn days. There is no solemnity so deep, to a right-thinking creature, as that of dawn. But not only in that beautiful sense, but in all their character and methods, they are to be solemn days... Every day of your early life is ordaining irrevocably, for good or evil, the custom and practice of your soul; ordaining either sacred customs of dear and lovely recurrence, or trenching deeper and deeper the furrows for seeds of sorrow. Now, therefore, see that no day passes in which you do not make yourself a somewhat better creature.

Do not look forward to what may happen tomorrow; the same everlasting 181-F-1
Father who cares for you today will take care of you tomorrow, and every day.

Take life too seriously, and what is it worth? If the morning wake us to no 81
new joys, if the evening bring us not the hope of new pleasures, is it worth while to dress and undress? Does the sun shine on me today that I may reflect on yesterday? That I may endeavor to foresee and to control what can neither be foreseen nor controlled—the destiny of tomorrow?

Life is short and we have not too much time for gladdening the hearts 6
of those who are traveling the dark way with us. Oh, be swift to love! Make haste to be kind!

I expect to pass through this world but once. Any good thing, therefore, 83
that I can do, or any kindness that I can show a fellow being, let me do it now. Let me not defer or neglect it, for I shall not pass this way again.

DAILY HELP

FOR DAILY NEEDS 175
Let thy blessing rest upon us, we pray. We praise thee for all thy good and perfect gifts. We know thy loving kindness will bestow upon us all things we truly need, and you will surely provide all those requirements for which we are most grateful.

This is the beginning of a new day. God has given me this day to use as I see fit. I can waste it or grow in its light and be of service to others. But what I do with this day is important because I have exchanged a day of my life for it. When tomorrow comes, today will be gone forever. I hope I do not regret the price I paid for it. 8

DAILY HINDU PRAYER 20-E
O Gods! All your names (and forms) are to be revered, saluted, and adored; all of you who have sprung from heaven, and earth, listen here to my invocation.

To heaven I lift my waiting eyes; 208
There all my hopes are laid;
The Lord that built the earth and skies
Is my perpetual aid.

Lord, help me live from day to day 147
In such a self-forgetful way,
That even when I kneel to pray,
My prayer shall be for... others.

DEATH and DYING

****

The absolute certainty, death, but also the eternal mystery... for it may be only a parting from those we love with a reunion in heaven for all eternity.

****

A PRAYER FOR DEATH 181-T-1

Absent from thee, my Saviour dear,
I call not life this living here,
But a long dying agony,
The sharpest I have ever known;
And I myself, myself to see
In such a wrack of misery,
For very pity moan;
And ever, ever, weep and sigh,
Crying because I do not die.

Ah! Lord, my light and living breath,
Take me, Oh, take me from this death,
And burst the bars that sever me
From my true life above!
Think how I die thy face to see,
And cannot live away from thee,
O my eternal Love.
And ever, ever, weep and sigh,
Dying, because I do not die.

Death stands above me, whispering low 124
I know not what into my ear;
Of his strange language all I know
Is, there is not a word of fear.

Lord, Jesus Christ, who knowest the hearts of men and who, in Thy Wisdom, didst create all things, grant that they, whom Thou didst visit in Thy wrath, may return to life; I beseech Thee, for the sake of them that are here present and are still seated in the darkness of error, to work this great wonder, that many may be strengthened in their faith, and others, illumined by its supernal light, may glorify Thy most Holy Name, now and forever. In the name of our Lord, Jesus Christ, who rose from the dead, arise and live! 181-E-2

What can they suffer that do not fear to die? 168

O Lord, support us all the day long, 157
until the shadows lengthen and the evening comes,
and the busy world is hushed, and the fever of life is over,
and our work is done.
Then in Thy mercy grant us a safe lodging, and a holy rest,
and peace at the last; through Jesus Christ our Lord.

Grant that we here before thee may be set free from the fear of vicissitude and the fear of death, may finish what remains before us of our course without dishonor to ourselves or hurt to others, and, when the day comes, may die in peace. 195

And bid me come to thee! 181-I-1
That with Thy saints I may praise Thee!
For ever and ever!

It is an exquisite and beautiful thing in our nature, that, when the heart is touched and softened by some tranquil happiness or affectionate feeling, the memory of the dead comes over it most powerfully and irresistibly. It would seem almost as though our better thoughts and sympathies were charms, in virtue of each the soul is enabled to hold some vague and mysterious intercourse with the spirits of those whom we loved in life. 57

FOR THE DEAD 157

Help, Lord, the soul which Thou hast made,
The soul to Thee so dear,
In prison for the debt unpaid
Of sins committed here.

Those holy souls, they suffer on,
Resign'd in heart and will,
Until Thy high behest is done,
And justice has its fill.
For daily falls, for pardon'd crime,
They joy to undergo
The shadow of Thy cross sublime,
The remnant of Thy woe.

Help, Lord, the soul which Thou hast made,
The soul to Thee so dear,
In prison for the debt unpaid
Of sins committed here.

Oh, by their patience of delay,
Their hope amid their pain,
Their sacred zeal to burn away
Disfigurement and stain;
Oh, by their fire of love, not less
In keenness than the flame,
Oh, by their very helplessness,
Oh by Thy own great Name,
Good Jesus, help! Sweet Jesus, aid
The souls to Thee most dear,
In prison for the debt unpaid
Of sins committed here.

DEATH and DYING

FOR A HOLY DEATH 175

O glorious Saint Paul, on earth thou wast a mirror of innocence and a model of penance. Thy life was spent in bringing back the erring souls of countless unfortunate sinners. Do mercifully look down once more from heaven and hear my petition. Obtain for me so great a love of Jesus that I may make His sufferings mine. Let me realize in the wounds of my Saviour the wickedness of my transgressions, and obtain from them, as from the fountain of salvation, the grace of bitter tears and a resolution to imitate thee in thy penance. Finally, intercede for me that I may, by the grace of God, die a holy death, and come at last to enjoy with thee His blessed presence in heaven for all eternity.

AT DEATH 181-P-3

Christ, unconquered King of glory!
Thou my wretched soul relieve
In that most extreme terror
When the body she must leave:
Let the accuser of the breathren
O'er me then no power receive!

Cowards die many times before their deaths: 186
The valiant never taste of death but once.
Of all the wonders that I yet have heard,
It seems to me most strange that man should fear;
Seeing that death, a necessary end,
Will come when it will come.

O Lord, Thou hast taken from us the fear of death; Thou makest the close of life, the commencement of a new and truer life. For a while Thou wilt suffer our bodies to sleep, and then will call us with the trumpet at the end of time. Now send Thee an angel of light beside me; bid him take my hand and lead me to the place of rest, where there is water for my thirst beside the dwelling place of the Holy Fathers. If in the weakness of the flesh I have sinned in word, or deed, or thought, forgive me Thou, O Lord, for Thou hast power to forgive sins on earth. When I am divested of my body, may I stand before Thee with my soul unspotted: receive it, Thou, without faults or sins, in Thine own hands. 141

Remind thyself that he whom thou lovest is mortal—that what thou lovest is not thine own, it is given thee for the present not irrevocably nor forever, but even as a fig or bunch of grapes at the appointed season of the year. 64

IN EXTREMIS 197

Lord, as from Thy body bleeding,
Wave by wave is life receding,
From these limbs of mine.
As it drifts away from me
To the everlasting sea,
Bind it, Lord, with Thine.

DEATH and DYING

PRAYER AT THE STAKE 181-J-2

Blessed Trinity, have mercy upon me!
Jesus, have pity upon me!
Virgin Mary, pray for me!
Blessed Saints of Paradise, pray for me!
Saint Michael, pray for me!
Saint Catherine, Saint Margaret, pray for me!
Whatever I have done, of good or evil, it is not my King who forced me to it. Whether you are of my party or against it, I most humbly ask your mercy.
I forgive you the harm you have done me. Please pray for me.

Catch the, O catch the transient hour; 115
Improve each moment as it flies;
Life's a short summer—mans a flower—
He dies—alas, how soon he dies!

There is a voice from the tomb sweeter than song; there is a remembrance 110
of the dead, to which we turn even from the charms of the living. These we would not exchange for the song of pleasure or the bursts of revelry.

IT IS A CURSE NEVER TO DIE 64

If heads of grain had feeling, ought they to pray that they should not be harvested? I would have you know that it is a curse never to die. The ship goes down. What, then, am I to do? Whatever I can. I drown without fear, neither shrinking nor crying out against God, but recognizing that what is born must also perish, for I am part of the whole, as an hour is part of a day. I must come on as the hour, and like an hour, pass away. Regard yourself as but a single thread of all that go to make up the garment. Seek not that the things which happen to you should be as you wish, but wish the things that happen to you to be as they are, and you will find tranquility.

FOR A PEACEFUL DEATH 175

O Jesus, you have known the anguish of my heart, the bitter agony of my spirit, and the suffering of my body. Help me in this hour. Though I walk through the shadow of death, I will fear no evil, for Thou art with me. I have comfort and consolation by Thy presence, hold my hand. Take my sins, which are many, and let thy grace sustain me. Lead me through my sorrow to the ultimate faith that I shall enter into joy everlasting.

Lord, my Creator, who didst guard me from my Childhood and enable 181-A-1
me, in my early youth, to act manfully; who didst take away from me the love of this vain world, and keep my body free from its defilement, who didst give me strength to overcome, and deem as naught the torments inflicted by the enemies of Thy Holy Name: I beseech Thee, receive this hour my soul into the hands of Thy mercy and bid me come onto Thee; O Thou, the sole desire and love of my heart.

DESPAIR

****

The darkness of despair can be banished from one's life by lighting the torches of faith, and hope, and love.

****

Beware of desperate steps; the darkest day, 48
Lived till tomorrow, will have passed away.

Times of great calamity and confusion have ever been productive of the greatest minds. The purest ore is produced from the hottest furnace, and the brightest thunderbolt is elicited from the darkest storm. 44

My God! in whom are all the springs 208
Of boundless love and grace unknown,
Hide me beneath Thy spreading wings,
Till the dark cloud is overblown.

Never despair; but if you do, work on in despair. 31

FROM PRISON 145
O Lord, my God, my hope is in Thee,
O Jesus, my dear one, do now set me free.
Bound to hard chains, in misery of grief
I still yearn for Thee.
Languishing, moaning, down on my knees
I worship and beg Thee to liberate me!

O God, I pray for help in my extreme need. The despair I feel has 175
blocked out all hope, all confidence, all faith in a just solution to this situation. Bring to me a spirit of trust and an optimistic attitude which will bring about an improvement of my circumstances. Thou knowest my needs and I pray for speedy assistance, along with a restoration of my knowledge that all things work for good when trust in your mercy is placed above all other thoughts.

O Lord God, ruler of heaven and of the earth, creator of things visible 143
and invisible, giver of eternal life, and consoler of the sorrowful, make me to stand firm in the confession of Thy name that as with Thine aid I have begun the good fight, so with Thine aid I may be deemed worthy to gain the victory, lest the adversary spitefully mock at me, saying: "Where is now her God in whom she trusted?" But let the angel of Thy light come and restore to me the light which the darkness of my cell has taken from me; and let the right hand of Thy majesty scatter the phantom hosts of the ancient enemy. For we know, O Lord, that Thy mercy will aid us in all temptations.

DISCIPLINE

****

Over 1,900 years ago, Epictetus said, "No man is free who is not master of himself." And, certainly we cannot aspire to influence others if we cannot control our own actions.

****

Govern thyself, and you will be able to govern the world. 170-A

It is true that we shall not be able to reach perfection, but in our struggle toward it we shall strengthen our characters and give stability to our ideas, so that, whilst ever advancing calmly in the same direction, we shall be rendered capable of applying the faculties with which we have been gifted to the best possible account. 45

How shall I be able to rule over others, 173
that have no full power and command of myself?

The glory of the star, the glory of the sun—we must not lose either in the other. We must not be so full of the hope of heaven that we cannot do our work on the earth; we must not be so lost in the work of the earth that we shall not be inspired by the hope of heaven. 24

Prosperity is a great teacher; adversity is a greater. 92
Possession pampers the mind, privation trains and strengthens it.

He who gains a victory over other men is strong; 125
but he who gains a victory over himself is all powerful.

SELF-CONTROL 9

Tost on a sea of troubles, Soul, my Soul,
Thyself do thou control;
And to the weapons of advancing foes
A stubborn breast oppose:
Undaunted mid the hostile might
Of squadrons burning for the flight.
Thine be no boasting when the victor's crown
Wins thee deserved renown;
Thine no dejected sorrow, when defeat
Would urge a base retreat:
Rejoice in joyous things - nor overmuch
Let grief thy bosom touch
Midst evil, and still bear in mind
How changeful are the ways of humankind.

EVENING

****
As the day draws to a close, it provides a tranquil time to pause and review the day, giving thanks for the gifts bestowed upon our lives since morning light.
****

GOOD NIGHT! 197

Good night, dear Lord! and now
Let them that loved to keep
Thy little bed in Bethlehem,
Be near me while I sleep;
For I—more helpless, Lord—of them
Have greater need than Thou.

Grant to me above all things that can be desired, to rest in Thee, 118
and in Thee to have my heart at peace.
Thou art the true peace of the heart, Thou its only rest;
out of Thee all things are hard and restless.
In this very peace, that is, in Thee,
the One Chiefest Eternal Good, I will sleep and rest.

A NIGHT PRAYER 8

May the will of God be done by us,
May the death of the saints be won by us,
And the lights of the kingdom begun in us;
May Jesus the Child be beside my bed,
May the Lamb of mercy uplift my head,
May the Virgin her heavenly brightness shed,
And Michael be steward of my soul!

Make a rule, and pray to God to help you keep it, never, if possible, to lie down at night without being able to say: "I have made one human being at least a little wiser, or a little happier, or at least a little better this day." 122

From EVENING HYMN 139

O God, whose daylight leadeth down
Into the sunless way,
Who with restoring sleep dost crown
The labor of the day!

What I have done, Lord, make it clean
With thy forgiveness dear;
That so to-day what might have been,
To-morrow may appear.

Close now thine eyes and rest secure; 172
Thy soul is safe enough, thy body sure;
He that love thee, he that keeps
And guards thee, never slumbers, never sleeps.

EVENING

ACHILD'S EVENING PRAYER 41

Ere on my bed my limbs I lay,
God grant me grace my prayers to say:
O God! preserve my mother dear
In strength and health for many a year;
And, O! preserve my father too,
And may I pay him reverence due;
And may I my best thoughts employ
To be my parents' hope and joy;
And, O! preserve my brothers both
From evil doings and from sloth,
And may we always love each other,
Our friends, our father, and our mother,
And still, O Lord, to me impart
An innocent and grateful heart,
That after my last sleep I may
Awake to thy eternal day!

Thou have kept me by your side this day, and I am truly grateful. Forgive whatever mistakes I've made and sins I've committed. Bless me this night with peaceful sleep so that I may serve Thee again tomorrow to the best of my abilities. 175

Watch, O Lord, with those who wake, or watch, 181-A-6
or weep tonight, and give your angels and saints
charge over those who sleep.
Tend your sick ones, O Lord Christ.
Rest your weary ones,
Bless your dying ones,
Soothe your suffering ones,
Pity your afflicted ones,
Shield your joyous ones,
And all for your love's sake.

When the day returns, call us up with morning faces and with morning hearts, eager to labor, happy if happiness be our portion, and if the day be marked for sorrow, strong to endure. 195

Lord, when we sleep let us not be afraid, but let our sleep be sweet, that we may be enabled to serve Thee on the morrow. 127

The man who says his prayers in the evening is a captain posting his sentires. After that, he can sleep. 15

EVIL

****

Just as any kindness done to another bears fruit, so also any evil thoughts or deeds return in kind. Remember always that love begets love, and that wrong-doing brings retribution in kind.

****

Save us from the evil tongue, 8
From the heart that thinketh wrong,
From the sins, whate'er they be,
That divide the soul from Thee.

Whenever evil befalls us, we ought to ask ourselves, after the first suffering, 107
how we can turn it into good. So shall we take occasion, from one bitter root, to raise perhaps many flowers.

All that is necessary for the triumph of evil is that good men do nothing. 31

Never let a man imagine that he can pursue a good end by evil means, 191
without sinning against his own soul. The evil effect on him is certain.

"Resist not evil" means "Do not resist the evil man," which is to say, 202
"Never offer violence to another," which is to say, "Never commit an act that is contrary to love."

A PRAYER 53

From falsehood and error,
From darkness and terror,
From all that is evil,
From the power of the devil,
From the fire and the doom,
From the judgment to come
Sweet Jesus, deliver
Thy servants forever.

This is a good universe. There is no permanent place in it for evil. Yea, 36
it would seem as if God and man and the universe itself were opposed to evil. Evil may hide behind this fallacy and that, but it will be hunted from fallacy to fallacy until there is no more fallacy for it to hide behind.

God made bees, and bees made honey, 8
God made man, and man made money,
Pride made the devil, and the devil made sin;
So God made a coal-pit to put the devil in.

For every evil under the sun, 8
There is a remedy or there is none.
If there is one, try to find it,
If there is none, never mind it.

FAITH

****

No better explanation of faith can be found than that of St. Augustine. "Faith is to believe, on the word of God, what we do not see, and its reward is to see and enjoy what we believe."

****

God enters by a private door into every individual. 63

FOR SEEKERS OF FAITH 181-B-3

Gracious and holy Father,
give us the wisdom to discover you,
the intelligence to understand you,
the diligence to seek after you,
the patience to wait for you,
eyes to behold you,
a heart to meditate on you,
and a life to proclaim you,
through the power of the spirit of Jesus, our Lord.

Faith is required of thee, and a sincere life, not loftiness of intellect, nor deepness in the mysteries of God. 118

If ye have faith as a grain of mustard seed, ye shall say unto this mountain: Remove hence to yonder place; and it shall remove. 20-A

Breathe on me, Breath of God. 88
Till I am wholly thine,
Till all this earthly part of me
Glows with thy fire divine.

Nothing in life is more wonderful than faith—the one great moving force we can neither weigh in the balance nor test in the crucible! 162

Lord, we have wandered forth through doubt and sorrow, 115
And Thou hast made each step an onward one;
And we will ever trust each unknown morrow,
Thou wilt sustain us till its work is done.

God is within us: He is that inner presence which makes us admire the beautiful, which rejoices us when we have done right and consoles us for not sharing the happiness of the wicked. 49

What your heart thinks great is great. The soul's emphasis is always right. 63

I am so glad! It is such rest to know 89
That Thou hast ordered and appointed all,
And wilt yet order and appoint my lot.
For though so much I cannot understand,
And would not choose, has been, and yet may be,
Thou choosest, Thou performest, Thou, my Lord.
This is enough for me.

FAITH

Give us, O Lord, a humble, quiet, peaceable, patient, tender and charity 181-T-4
able mind, and may all our thoughts, words, and deeds have a taste of Thy
Holy Spirit. Give us, O Lord, a lively faith, a firm hope, a fervent charity,
a love of Thee. Take from us all lukewarm ness in meditation, dullness in
prayer. Give us tender compassion towards us. The things, good Lord that
we pray for give us grace to labor for; through Jesus Christ our Lord.

He that has lost faith, what has he left to live on? 13

All my life I still have found, 79
And I will forget it never;
Every sorrow hath its bound,
And no cross endures forever.
All things else have but their day,
God's love only lasts for aye.

God shall be my hope, 186
My stay, my guide and lantern to my feet.

PRAYER OF AFFIRMATION 137
A mighty fortress is our God, A bulwark never failing;
Our helper He amid the flood of mortal ills prevailing;
For still our ancient toe doth seek to work us woe;
His craft and power are great, and, armed with cruel hate,
On earth is not his equal.

Did we in our strength confide, Our striving would be losing;
Were not the right man on our side, The man of God's own choosing;
Dost ask who that may be? Christ Jesus, it is He,
Lord Sabaoth His name, From age to age the same,
And he must win the battle.

And though this world, with devils filled, should threaten to undo us;
We will not fear, for God hath willed His truth to triumph through us.
The Prince of darkness grim, we tremble not for Him;
His rage we can endure, for lo! His doom is sure,
One little word shall fell him.

That word above all earthly powers, No thanks to them, abideth;
The Spirit and the gifts are ours through Him who with us sideth;
Let goods and kindred go, This mortal life also;
The body they may kill; God's truth abideth still,
His kingdom is forever.

He does not believe who does not live according to his belief. 76

The person who has a firm trust in the Supreme Being is powerful in 2
his power, wise by his wisdom, happy by his happiness.

FAITH

OUT OF THE DEPTHS 123

Torn upon Thy wheel,
Foul'd with blood and dust,
Still my heart can feel,
Still trust;

Still my lips can urge,
"Heal me with Thy sword,
Cleanse me with Thy scourge,
Lord, Lord!"

Though a bleeding clod,
Faint and thirst and pain,
Still my hopes, dear God,
Remain;

Yea, and more than hope:
Faith! A prayer! A wing!
Even on Calvary's slope,
I sing!

In Thee I place my trust, 138
On Thee I calmly rest;
I know Thee good, I know Thee just,
And count Thy choice the best.

In all my perplexities and distresses, the Bible has never failed to give 129
me light and strength.

FAITH IS IN THE HEART 165

The heart has its reasons, which reason does not know. We feel it in a thousand things. I say that the heart naturally loves the Universal Being, and also itself naturally, according as it gives itself to them; and it hardens itself against one or the other at its will. You have rejected the one, and kept the other. Is it by reason that you love yourself?

It is the heart which experiences God, and not the reason. This then, is faith: God felt by the heart, not by the reason.

Faith is a gift of God; do not believe that we said it was a gift of reasoning. Other religions do not say this of their faith. They only give reasoning in order to arrive at it, and yet it does not bring them to it.

But give me, Lord, eyes to behold the truth; 164
A seeing sense that knows the eternal right;
A heart with pity filled, and gentlest truth;
A manly faith that makes all darkness light.

All I have seen teaches me to trust the Creator for all I have not seen. 63

FAITH

Come perfect Sun of heaven's love, 181-A-2
In lasting radiance from above.
And pour the Spirit's cloudless ray
On all we think or do today.

Confirm our will to do the right,
And keep our hearts from evil's blight;
Let faith her eager fires renew,
And hate the false and love the true.

Thy path is plain and straight—that light is given: 191
Onward in faith—and leave the rest to Heaven.

Lord, purge our eyes to see 178
Within the seed a tree,
Within the glowing egg a bird,
Within the shell a butterfly.

Till taught by such, we see
Beyond all creatures Thee,
And hearken to Thy tender word,
And hear it, "Fear not, it is I."

Speak, Lord, for thy servant hearth. Grant us ears to hear, eyes to see, wills to obey, hearts to love; then declare what Thou wilt, reveal what Thou wilt, command what Thou wilt, and demand what Thou wilt. 178

O Lord, whose way is perfect, help us, we pray Thee, always to trust in Thy goodness; that, walking with Thee and following Thee in all simplicity, we may possess quiet and contented minds, and may cast all care on Thee, for Thou carest for us. 178

We have but faith: we cannot know: 200
For knowledge is of things we see;
And yet we trust it comes from thee,
A beam in darkness: let it grow.

O Lord Jesus Christ, give us such a measure of thy spirit that we may be enabled to obey thy teaching: To pacify anger, to take part in pity, to moderate desire, to increase love, to put away sorrow, to cast away vain-glory; not to be vindictive, not to fear death; ever entrusting our spirit to immortal God, who with thee and the Holy Ghost liveth and reigneth world without end. 181-A-5

I believe in God the Father Almighty because wherever I have looked, through all that I see around me, I see the trace of an intelligent mind, and because in natural laws, and especially in the laws which govern the social relations of man, I see, not merely the proofs of intelligence, but the proofs of beneficence. 78

FAITH AND CONTENT 84

My Lord, how full of sweet content,
I pass my years of banishment!
Where'er I dwell, I dwell with Thee,
In Heaven, in earth, or on the sea.

To me remains nor place nor time;
My country is in every clime;
I can be calm and free from care
On any shore, since God is there.

To believe is to be strong. Doubt cramps energy. Belief is power. 176

O merciful Lord, enlighten Thou me with a clear shining inward light, 118
and remove away all darkness from the habitation of my heart. Repress Thou my many wandering thoughts, and break in pieces those temptations which violently assault me. Fight Thou for me, and vanquish the evil beasts; that so peace may be obtained by Thy power, and that Thine abundant praise may resound in Thy holy court, that is, in a pure conscience. Send out Thy light and Thy truth, that they may shine upon the earth; for, until Thou enlighten me, I am but as earth without form and void. Lift Thou up my mind which is pressed down by a load of sins, for no created thing can give full comfort and rest to my desires. Join Thou me to Thyself with an inseparable band of love; for Thou even alone dost satisfy him that loveth Thee.

TO INCREASE ONE'S FAITH 181-B-4

O Jesus, Light of all below,
Thou Fount of life and fire,
Surpassing all the joys we know,
And all we can desire!

May every heart confess Thy name,
And ever Thee adore;
And seeking Thee, itself inflame
To seek Thee more and more.

Thee may our tongues for ever bless;
Thee may we love alone;
And ever in our lives express
The image of Thine own.

Renew Thine image, Lord, in me
79
Lowly and gently may I be;
No charms but these to Thee are dear;
No anger mayst Thou ever find.
No pride in my unruffled mind,
But faith and heaven born peace be there.

FAITH

We live by Faith; but Faith is not the slave 211
Of test and legend. Reason's voice and Gods,
Nature's and Duty's, never are at odds.

Thy thoughts are good, and Thou art kind, 79
E'en when we think it not;
How many an anxious, faithless mind
Sits grieving o'er its lot,
And frets, and pines by day and night,
As God had lost it out of sight,
And all its wants forgot.

Faith is a certain image of eternity. All things are present in it—things past, and things to come; it converses with angels, and antedates the hymns of glory. Every man that hath this grace is as certain there are glories for him, if he perseveres in duty, as if he had heart and sung the thanksgiving song for the blessed sentence of doomsday. 198

I look to Thee in every need, 134
And never look in vain;
I feel Thy touch, Eternal Love,
And all is well again:
The thought of Thee is mightier far
Than sin and pain and sorrow are.

Faith is one of the forces by which men live, and the total absence of it means collapse. 112

O gentle Jesus, I implore thee to set me on fire with a burning love of God. Obtain for me, I pray, this grace from God which will enrich my life here on earth and make me worthy to be united with God forever in heaven. 175

Beware of despairing about yourself: you are commanded to put your trust in God, and not in yourself. 181-A-6

We shall steer safely through every storm, so long as our heart is right, our intention fervent, our courage steadfast, and our trust fixed on God. If at times we are somewhat stunned by the tempest, never fear. Let us take breath, and go on afresh. 181-F-1

Faith is not merely praying 8
Upon our knees at night;
Faith is not merely straying
Through darkness into light;
Faith is not merely waiting
For glory that may be.
Faith is the brave endeavor,
The splendid enterprise,
The strength to serve, whatever
Conditions may arise.

****

A close knit, loving family is the desire of all of us. If you have it, you are among the most fortunate. But if this gift it not one of your blessings, do not be bitter. Look around-there is many people who would like to be your friend. Take the first step; reach out to someone who may be as lonely as you. Do it now and a year from today you will be glad you took my advice.

****

THE HOUSE BEAUTIFUL 8

The Crown of the house is Godliness.
The Beauty of the house is Order.
The Glory of the house is Hospitality.
The Blessing of the house is Contentment.

PRAYER FOR FAMILY BLESSING 195

Lord, behold our family here assembled. We thank Thee for this place in which we dwell; for the love that united us; for the peace accorded us this day; for the hope with which we expect the morrow; for the health, the work, the food, and the bright skies, that make our lives delightful; for our friends in all parts of the earth, and our friendly helpers in this foreign isle. Let peace abound in our small company.

Purge out of every heart the lurking grudge. Give us grace and strength to forebear and persevere. Offenders, give us the grace to accept and to forgive offenders. Forgetful ourselves, help us to bear cheerfully the gleefulness of others. Give us courage and gaiety and the quiet mind. Spare us to our friends, soften to us our enemies. Bless us, if it may be, in all our innocent endeavors. If it may not, give us the strength to encounter that which is to come, that we may be brave in peril, constant in tribulation, temperate in wrath, and in all changes of fortune down to gates of death, loyal, and loving one to another. As the clay to the potter, as the windmill to the wind, as children of their sire, we beseech of Thee the help and mercy, for Christ's sake.

A PRAYER 187

It is my joy in life to find
At every turning of the road
The strong arm of a comrade kind
To help me onward with my load.

The only way to have a friend is to be one. 63

He is the happiest, be he king or peasant, who finds peace in his home. 81

There is magic in that little word, home; it is a mystic circle that surrounds comforts and virtues never known beyond its hallowed limits. 191

This fond attachment to the well-known place whence first we started into life's long race, maintains its hold with such unfailing sway, we feel it e'en in age, and at our latest day. 48

FEAR

****
Many live by the motto which says, "It's good to worry, for the things I worry about never seem to happen." Ah, but think of all the time which has been wasted by the worrying when those fears would never have materialized at all.
****

Fear not that thy life shall come to an end, but rather fear that it shall never have a beginning. 157

BORROWING 63

Some of your hurts you have cured,
And the sharpest you still have survived,
But what torments of grief you endured
From evil which never arrived!

Keep your fears to yourself but share your courage with others. 195

A man's own conscience is his sole tribunal, and he should care no more for that phantom "opinion" than he should fear meeting a ghost if he crossed the churchyard at dark. 29

I take Thy hand, and fears grow still; 115
Behold Thy face, and doubts remove;
Who would not yield his wavering will
To perfect Truth, and boundless Love?

Fear only two: God and the man who has no fear of God. 170-B

Let us be of good cheer, remembering that the misfortunes hardest to bear are those which never happen. 135

Beware of desperate steps; the darkest day, 48
Lived till tomorrow, will have passed away.

If, when you look into your own heart, you find nothing wrong there, what is there to worry about, what is there to fear? 45

Blessed Jesus, I ask for your blessing that I may eliminate from my life anxiety and fears. The past is gone and cannot be changed, tomorrow is not yet here and should not claim my attentions. It is to this day only I am responsible. With God, around me, protecting me, I will banish the gloom of fear which darkens my way and leads me to stumble into error. 175

FOR OTHERS

****

To offer petitions on behalf of others is truly a noble and uplifting purpose. It becomes a gift for both giver and receiver, always bringing untold blessings.

****

FOR ALL MANKIND 181-C-4

"God of all flesh, who qivest life and death,
thou who castest down the insolence of the proud and turnest
aside the scheming of men, be our help!
Oh, Master, appease the hunger of the indigent;
Deliver the fallen among us.
God, good and merciful, forget our sins,
our wrongdoing and backsliding;
take no account of the faults of thy servants.
Give us concord and peace, as to all the inhabitants of the earth.
It is from thee that our princes and those who govern us
here below hold their power;
grant them health, peace, concord, stability;
direct their counsels in the way of goodness.
Thou alone canst do all this and-confer on us still greater benefits.
We proclaim it by the high priest and master of our soul, Jesus Christ,
by whom to thee be all glory and power, now and in endless ages."

Pray for others in such forms, with such length, importunity, and earnestness, as you use for yourself; and you will find all little, ill-natured passions die away, your heart grow great and generous, delighting in the common happiness of others, as you need only to delight in your own. 128

FOR THE SICK 175

O God, look down from heaven and grant thy servant the help of thy power that, according to thy good pleasure, the sickness may be turned into health, and the sorrow into joy. Look down in mercy, bestow thy comfort, and instill such confidence in thy healing hands.

FOR THE POOR 181-A-6

O Lord, Who, though Thou wast rich, yet for our sakes didst become poor, and hast promised in Thy gospel that whatsoever is done unto the least of Thy brethren, Thou wilt receive as done unto Thee; give us grace, we humbly beseech Thee, to be ever willing and ready to minister, as Thou enablest us, to the necessities of our fellow creatures, and to extend the blessings of Thy kingdom over all the world, to Thy praise and glory, Who art God over all, blessed for ever.

I pray for those who love me 8
Whose hearts are kind and true.
For the Heaven that smiles above me,
And awaits my spirit too.
For all human ties that bind me,
For the task God has assigned me,
For the bright hopes yet to find me,
And for the good that I can do.

FOR OTHERS

We bring before Thee, O Lord, the troubles and perils of people 181-A-3
and nations, the sighing of prisoners and captives,
the sorrows of the bereaved,
the necessities of strangers,
the helplessness of the weak,
the despondency of the weary,
the failing powers of the aged.
O Lord, draw near to each; for the sake of Jesus Christ our Lord.

For our absent loved ones we implore thy loving kindness. Keep them 195
in life, keep them in growing honor; and for us, grant that we remain
worthy of their love. For Christ's sake, let not our beloved blush for us,
or we for them. Grant us but that, and grant us courage to endure lesser
ills unshaken, and to accept death, loss, and disappointment as if it were
straws upon the tide of life.

FOR ENEMIES 181-T-4
Almighty God, have mercy on all that bear me evil will,
and would me harm, and their faults and mine together,
by such easy, tender, merciful means as Thy infinite wisdom can
divine, vouchsafe to amend and redress,
and make us saved souls in heaven together where we may ever live
and love together with Thee and Thy blessed saints,
O Glorious Trinity, for the bitter passion of our sweet Savior Christ.

I would that the loving were loved, and 154
I would that the weary should sleep,
And that man should hearken to man,
And that he that soweth should reap.

Bless, we pray Thee, all for whom we should pray. We name them in 175
the silence of our hearts. Pity the ungrateful, the wayward, and the
wanderer. Comfort the lonely and desolate. Let Thy peace rule in all our
hearts and in our homes. When we stumble, may Thy strength support us,
Thy wisdom leads us, Thy love redeems us. Open our hearts to all that is
good and loving. We ask this in Thy Holy Name.

FOR DELIVERANCE FROM TROUBLE 175
We ask Thee, God, to look with pity upon all who are in need or trouble,
and come and help them. Strengthen the weak, succor those who are
tempted, lift up the fallen, lighten the darkness of them in doubt, give
patience to all who suffer, and to them who are disheartened grant
needed courage and new interest in life.

The only religion that will do anything toward enriching your life is the 8
religion which inspires you to do something toward enriching the life of
others.

****

It is not for others that we must forgive, but for ourselves. Forgiveness saves much—anger, resentment, hatred, and waste of the spirit.

****

FORGIVENESS AND MERCY 177

Jesus Christ, have mercy on me,
As thou art king of majesty.

And forgive me my sins all
That I have done both great and small.

And bring me, if it be thy will,
Till heaven, to live aye with thee still.

Since I myself stand in need of God's pity, I granted an amnesty to all my enemies. 94

Out of the depths have I cried unto thee, O Lord. 20-A
Lord, hear my voice: let thine ears be attentive to the voice of
my supplications. If thou, Lord, shouldest mark iniquities,
O Lord, who shall stand?
But there is forgiveness with thee, that thou mayest be feared.
I wait for the Lord, my soul doth wait, and in his word do I hope.

TIMES WITHOUT NUMBER HAVE I PRAY'D 209

Times without number have I prayed,
"This only once forgive";
Relapsing, when Thy hand was stayed.
And suffered me to live:

Yet now the kingdom of Thy peace,
Lord, to my heart restore;
Forgive my vain repentances,
And bid me sin no more.

Only the brave know how to forgive; it is the most refined and generous pitch of virtue that human nature can arrive at. 194

Tis not enough to weep my sins, 68
Tis but one step to heaven:
When I am kind to others, then
I know myself forgiven.

The more we know, the better we forgive; 193
Who'er feels deeply, feels for all who live.

The noblest revenge is to forgive. 76

FORGIVENESS

REMEMBER NOT, LORD, MY SINS 7

Remember not, Lord, my sins,
Not the sins of my forefathers;
Neither take vengeance for our sins, theirs, nor mine.
Spare us, Lord, them and me,
Spare Thy people,
And, among Thy people, Thy servant,
Who is redeemed with Thy previous blood;
And be not angry with us forever.
Be merciful, be merciful; spare us, Lord,
And be not angry with us, forever.
Be merciful, be merciful; have pity on us, Lord,
And be not angry with us to the full.
Deal not, O Lord,
Deal not with me after mine iniquities,
Neither recompense me according to my sins;
But after Thy great pity,
Deal with me,
And according to the multitude of Thy mercies,
Recompense me
After that so great pity,
And that multitude of mercies,
As Thou didst to our fathers
In the times of old—
by all that is dear unto Thee.

O Lord, who has mercy upon all, 181-A-2
Take away from me my sins,
And mercifully kindle in me the fire of Thy Holy Spirit.
Take away from me the heart of stone,
And give me a heart of flesh,
A heart to love and adore Thee,
A heart to delight in Thee,
To follow and to enjoy Thee, for Christ's sake.

From the murmur and subtlety of suspicion with which we vex one another, give us rest. 10

Make a new beginning and mingle again the kindred of the nations in the alchemy of love,

And with some fine essence of forbearance temper our minds.

O Holy Child of Bethlehem, 24
Descend to us, we pray;
Cast out our sins, and enter in,
Be born in us today.

He that cannot forgive others, breaks the bridge over which he himself must pass if he would ever reach heaven, for every one has need to be forgiven. 97

FORGIVENESS

DELIVERANCE FROM SIN 167
O Lord God! Thou lovest holiness, and purity is thy delight in the earth. Wherefore, I pray thee, make an end of sin, and finish transgression, and bring in thy everlasting righteousness to the souls of men, that thy poor creation may be delivered from the bondage it groans under, and the earth enjoy her sabbath again: That thy great name may be lifted up in all nations; and thy salvation renowned to the ends of the world. For thine is the kingdom, the power, and the glory forever.

Blessed Apostle Peter, to whom God has given the keys of the kingdom 175
of heaven, and the power to bind and loose; grant that we may be delivered, through the help of intercession, from the bonds of our sins.

Search me, O God, and know my heart; try me, and know my thoughts; 20-A
and see if there be any wicked way in me, and lead me in the way everlasting.

O Thou who coverest Thyself with light as with a garment, shine Thou in us, 164
putting to flight all the forces of darkness and guilt, of sin and selfishness. Shine also through us to any that live in shadow, and so fill us with Thy radiant spirit that we may be a lamp unto a neighbor's feet and a light up to his path. And when this day is done, may every face we have met be the brighter for our meeting, and every heart braver, with new joy and cheer and grace and strength.

A PRAYER 139

When I look back upon my life nigh spent,
Nigh spent, although the stream as yet flows on,
I more of follies than of sins repent,
Less for offence than Love's shortcomings moan,
With self, O Father, leave me not alone-
Leave not with the beguiler, the beguiled;
Besmirched and ragged, Lord, take back thine own:
A fool I bring thee to be made a child.

Good to forget- 26
Best to forgive!

The kindest and the happier pair 48
Will find occasion to forbear;
And something, every day they live,
To pity, and perhaps forgive.

And if we do but watch the hour 33
There never yet was human power
Which could evade, if unforgiving,
The patient search and vigil long
Of him who treasures up a wrong.

FORGIVENESS

HIS PRAYER FOR ABSOLUTION 98

For those my unbaptized Rhimes,
Writ in my wild unhallowed Times;
For every sentence, clause and word,
That's not inlaid with Thee, my Lord.
Forgive me God and blot each Line
Out of my Book, that is not Thine.
But if, amongst all, thou find'st here one
Worthy thy Benediction;
That One of all the rest, shall be
The Glory of my Work and Me.

God forgives sins committed against Him, but offenses against man must first be forgiven by the injured person. 20-G

From THE POET'S JOURNAL 198

God, to whom we look up blindly,
look Thou down upon us kindly:
We have sinned, but not designedly.

If our faith in Thee was shaken,
Pardon Thou our hearts mistaken,
Our obedience reawaken.

We are Sinful, Thou art holy:
Thou art mighty, we are lowly:
Let us reach Thee, climbing slowly.

Our ingratitude confessing,
On Thy mercy still transgressing,
Thou dost punish us with blessing!

BEFORE COMMUNION 8

O Savior, who lightest the sun's blessed ray,
Remit my offenses, this day and always,
Above my deserving, or all I could pay;
Then with joy I receive my Redeemer today.

Merciful God, receive this humble prayer and send down plentiful showers of divine favors. By the fire of love in thy heart, obtain for us the mercies of pardon and remission of all our sins, steadfastness in faith, and perseverance in good works, so that we may become worthy of thy powerful patronage. 175

Extend thy protection to our bodies also, and deliver us from sickness. Obtain from God through thine intercession the healing of our spiritual maladies. Let thy heart be tender toward us, O mighty God. Stretch forth thy hand over us, and obtain for us those graces for the welfare of both soul and body, which we so earnestly ask of thee.

GRACE

****

Shakespeare wrote that "The king-becoming graces are justice, verity, temperance, stableness, bounty, perseverance, mercy, lowliness, devotion, patience, courage, fortitude." Oh, that we could attain them all. Shall we start?

****

THREEFOLD GRACE 104

Grant me dear Lord for this year's term I pray
A threefold grace to sanctify each day:
Grace so to guide and to control my tongue
That none by it may be misled or stung.
Grace to detach myself from worldly snares,
From trivial talk and worrying Martha cares.
Grace in adoring love to take my seat
Like Mary, meek and silent at Thy feet.

GRACE 63

How much, preventing God, how much I owe
To the defenses thou hast round me set;
Example, custom, fear, occasion slow,
These scorned bondmen were my parapet.
I dare not peep over their parapet
To gauge with glance the roaring gulf below,
The depths of sin to which I had descended,
Had not these me against myself defended.

Plenteous grace with Thee is found, 209
Grace to cover all my sin;
Let the healing streams abound;
Make and keep me pure within.

Whatever is graceful is virtuous, and whatever is virtuous is graceful. 40

A GRACE 8

Great Giver of the open hand,
We stand to thank Thee for our meat,
A hundred praises, Christ, 'tis meet,
For all we drink, for all we eat.

FOR GRACE 195

Grant that we here before Thee may be set free from the fear of vicissitude and the fear of death, may finish what remains before us of our course without dishonor to ourselves or hurt to others, and, when the day comes, may die in peace. Deliver us from fear and favor: from mean hopes and cheap pleasures. Have mercy on each in his deficiency; let him be not cast down; support the stumbling on the way, and give at last rest to the weary.

GRATITUDE

****

Shame on those who deny their blessings ... you are alive ... you have eyes to see wondrous things ... you have work to do ... you are not hungry ... you are not in pain ... you care for someone ... and someone cares for you.

****

GRATEFUL HEART 97

Thou hast given so much to me,
Give me one thing more - a grateful heart;
Not thankful when it pleaseth me,
As if Thy blessings had spare days;
But such a heart, whose pulse may be
Thy praise.

A good deed is never lost. He who sows courtesy, reaps friendship; he who plants kindness, gathers love; pleasure bestowed upon a grateful mind was never sterile, but generally gratitude begets reward. 181-B-1

Act with kindness, but do not expect gratitude. 45

We thank Thee for all the gifts that come from Thy liberal hand; for life, and health, and friends, and home. We thank Thee for Thy protection and care while we sleep, and for the new mornings with its call to work; for the food and clothing so freely provided; and for the shelter and peace of the home. Guide and direct us this day in all that we do, that we may be kind and loving in all our relationship with other people. 175

Since we cannot get what we like, let us like what we can get. 170-H

He is a wise man who does not grieve for the things which he has not, but rejoices for those which he has. 64

O our God, bestow upon us such confidence, such peace, such happiness in Thee, that Thy will may always be dearer to us than our own will, and Thy pleasure than our own pleasure. All that Thou givest is Thy free gift to us; all that Thou takest away is Thy grace to us. Be Thou thanked for all, praised for all, loved for all; through Jesus Christ our Lord. 178

I thank Thee for a daily task to do, 8
For books that are my ships with golden wings,
For mighty gifts let others offer praise--
Lord, I am thanking Thee for little things.

If a man carries his cross beautifully and makes it radiant with glory of a meek and gentle spirit, the time will come when the things that now disturb will be the events for which he will most of all give gratitude to God. 8

GRATITUDE

An easy thing, O Power Divine, 99
To thank Thee for these gifts of Thine,
For summer's sunshine, winter's snow,
For hearts that kindle, thoughts that glow;
But when shall I attain to this -
To thank Thee for the things I miss?

Lord, we thank Thee for this place in which we dwell; for the love that 195
unites us; for the peace accorded us this day; for the hope with which
we expect the morrow; for the health, the work, the food, and the bright
skies that make our lives delightful; for our friends in all parts of the earth,
and our friendly helpers. Give us grace and strength to forbear and to
persevere. Give us courage and gaiety and the quiet mind. Spare to us our
friends, soften to us our enemies. Bless us, if it may be, in all our innocent
endeavors. If it may not, give us strength to encounter that which is to
come, that we be brave in peril, constant in tribulation, temperate in
wrath, and in all changes of fortune, and down to the gates of death, loyal
and loving to one another.

Lord, when I look upon mine own life it seems Thou hast led me so 181-A-6
carefully, so tenderly, Thou canst have attended to no one else; but when
I see how wonderfully Thou hast led the world and art leading it, I am
amazed that Thou hast time to attend to such as I.

We are evil, O God, and help us to see it and amend. We are good, and 195
help us to be better. Look down upon thy servants with a patient eye, even
as thou sendest sun and rain; look down, call up the dry bones, quicken,
enliven; recreate in us the soul of service, the spirit of peace; renew in us
the sense of joy.

Let not your mind run on what you lack as much as on what you have 12
already. Of the things you have, select the best; and then reflect how
eagerly they would have been sought if you did not have them.

Father, we thank Thee for the night, 8
And for the pleasant morning light;
For rest and food and loving care,
And all that makes the day so fair.

O Thou, who kindly dost provide 32
For every creature's want!
We bless Thee, God of nature wide,
For all Thy goodness lent:
And, if it please Thee, heavenly Guide,
May never worse be sent;
But, whether granted or denied,
Lord, bless us with content!

GRATITUDE

It is another's fault if he is ungrateful, but it is mine if I do not give. 185
To find one thankful man, I will oblige a great many that are not so.

Without Thy sunshine and Thy rain 8
We could not have the golden grain;
Without Thy love we'd not be fed;
We thank Thee for our daily bread.

Epicurus says, "Gratitude is a virtue that has commonly profit annexed 185
to it." And where is the virtue that has not? But, still the virtue is to be
valued for itself, and not for the profit that attends it.

If you can't be thankful for what you receive, be thankful for what you 8
escape.

May silent thanks at least to God be given with a full heart; 215
Our thoughts are heard in heaven.

Let never day nor night unhallowed pass, 186
But still remember what the Lord hath done.

From David learn to give thanks for everything. Every furrow in the 199
Book of Psalms is sown with the seeds of Thanksgiving.

THANKSGIVING 103

Lord, for the erring thought
Not into evil wrought;
Lord, for the wicked will,
Betrayed and baffled still;
For the heart from itself kept,
Our thanksgivings accept!
For ignorant hopes that were
Broken at our blind prayer;
For pain, death, sorrow sent,
Unto our chastisement;
For all loss of seeming good,
Quicken our gratitude.

For the few hours of life allotted me, 47
Give me but bread and liberty,
I'll beg no more; if more thou art pleased to give,
I'll thankfully that over plus receive;
If beyond this no more be freely sent,
I'll thank for this, and go away content.

A thankful heart is not only the greatest virtue, but the parent of all 40
the other virtues.

GRATITUDE

Make a joyful noise unto the Lord, all ye lands. 20-A
Serve the Lord with gladness: come before his presence with singing. Know ye that the Lord he is God: it is he that hath made us, and not we ourselves; we are his people, and the sheep of his pasture. Enter into his gates with thanksgiving, and into his courts with praise: be thankful unto him, and bless his name. For the Lord is good; his mercy is everlasting; and his truth endureth to all generations.

Were there no God we would be in this glorious world with grateful hearts; and no one to thank. 178

THANKSGIVING 63

For each new morning with its light,
Father, we thank Thee.
F or rest and shelter of the night,
Father, we thank Thee.
For health and food, for love and friends,
For everything Thy goodness sends,
Father, in heaven, we thank Thee.

GRIEF and SORROW

****
There is no escaping grief for it is as much a part of life as joy, when it comes, bear it. Keeping in mind that it will pass for time is a great healer.
****

Endure and persist; this pain will turn to your good. 163

THE RAINY DAY 134

The day is cold, and dark, and dreary;
It rains, and the wind is never weary;
The vine still clings to the moldering wall,
But at every gust the dead leaves fall,
And the day is dark and dreary.

My life is cold, and dark, and dreary;
It rains, and the wind is never weary;
My thoughts still cling to the moldering past,
But the hopes of youth fall thick in the blast,
And the days are dark and dreary.

Be still sad heart! And cease repining;
Behind the clouds the sun is still shining
Thy fate is the common fate of all,
Into each life some rain must fall,
Some days must be dark and dreary.

Sorrow is given us on purpose to cure us of sin. 181-J-3

You cannot prevent the birds of sorrow from flying over your head, but you can prevent them from building nests in your hair. 170-A

Sorrow is the mere rust of the soul. Activity will cleanse and brighten it. 115

CONSOLATION 157

When I sink down in gloom or fear,
Hope blighted or delayed,
Thy whisper, Lord, my heart shall cheer,
"'Tis I, be not afraid!"

Or startled at some sudden blow,
If fretful thoughts I feel,
"Fear not, it is but I" shall flow,
As balm my wound to heal.

There is no grief which time does not lessen and soften. 40

Not to have had pain is not to have been human. 170-I

GRIEF and SORROW

WEEP NO MORE 70

Weep no more, nor sigh nor groan,
Sorrow call no time that's gone:
Violets pluck'd, the sweetest rain
Makes not fresh, nor grow again;
Trim thy locks look cheerfully,
Fate's hidden ends eyes cannot see.
Joys as winged dreams fly fast,
Why should sadness longer last?
Grief is hut a wound to woe;
Gentlest fair, mourn, mourn no more.

FOR SOLACE 181-T-1

O my Lord,
when I think in how many ways Thou hast suffered,
and that Thou didst in no wise deserve it,
I do not know what to say for myself,
nor of what I am thinking when I shrink from suffering,
nor where I am when I excuse myself.
O Jesus, Thou brightness of eternal glory,
solace of the pilgrim soul.
with Thee is my mouth without voice,
and my silence speaks to Thee.

Go, bury thy sorrow. The world hath its share; 8
Go, bury it deeply. Go, hide it with care.
Go, bury thy sorrow. Let others be blest;
Go, give them the sunshine. And tell God the rest.

May this burden of grief, sorrow, and suffering be lifted from my aching heart. Replace these afflictions with the healing love which will lift me out of my despair. Banish bitterness from my mind and turn my sad thoughts toward happy memories, gratitude for the good which remains in my life, and the serenity with which to go forward to a truly happier future. 175

Silence is no certain token 89
That no secret grief is there;
Sorrow which is never spoken
Is the heaviest load to bear.

Oh, then indulge thy grief, nor fear to tell 48
The gentle source from whence thy sorrows flow!
Nor think it weakness when we love to feel,
Nor think it weakness what we feel to show.

GUIDANCE

****

What to do? When to do it? How to work it out? Why am I in this mess? The answers will come through prayer and patience, and by keeping busy at constructive employment while waiting for the guidelines you are searching for.

****

FOR GUIDANCE 80

O Master, let me walk with Thee
In lowly paths of service free;
Tell me Thy secret; help me bear
The strain of toil, the fret of care.

Help me the slow of heart to move
By some clear winning word of love.
Teach me the wayward feet to stay,
And guide them in the homeward way.

Teach me Thy patience; still with Thee
In closer, dearer company,
In work that keeps faith sweet and strong,
In trust that triumphs over wrong;

In hope that sends a shining ray
Far down the future's broadening way;
In peace that only Thou canst give,
With Thee, O Master, let me live.

Lord God, king of heaven and earth, 8
this day, direct, rule and govern
my mind, my heart, body, thoughts, words, and deeds
so that now and forever more
I may experience salvation and true freedom.
O Savior of the world, help me.

Make use of me for the future as Thou wilt. 64
I am of the same mind; I am one with Thee.
I refuse nothing which seems good to Thee.
Lead me whither Thou wilt, cloth me in whatever dress Thou wilt.
Is it Thy will that I should be in a public or a private condition,
dwell here, or be banished, be poor or rich?
Under all these circumstances, I will testify unto Thee before men.

Almighty God, the Giver of all good things, 115
without Whose help all labor is ineffectual,
and without Whose grace all wisdom is folly,
grant we beseech Thee, that in all our undertakings,
Thy Holy Spirit may not be withheld from us;
but that we may promote Thy glory,
and the salvation both of ourselves and others.
Grant this, O Lord, for the sake of Jesus Christ our Lord.

GUIDANCE

O Lord, may I be directed what to do and what to leave undone and 75
then may I humbly trust that a blessing will be with me in my various engagements.

Enable me, O Lord, to feel tenderly and charitably toward all my beloved fellow mortals. Help me to have no soreness or improper feelings toward any. Let me think no evil, bear all things, hope all things, endure all things.

Let me walk in all humility and Godly fear before all men and in Thy sight.

O Lord my God, do Thou Thy holy will, I will lie still. 117
I will not stir, lest I forsake Thine Arm, and break the charm
Which lulls me, clinging to my Father's breast, in perfect rest.

My Father! What am I, that all 8
Thy mercies sweet like sunlight fall
So constant over my way?
That Thy great love should shelter me,
And guide my steps so tenderly
Through every changing day?

O Lord, I give myself to Thee, I trust Thee wholly. 157
Thou art wiser than I, more loving to me than I myself.
Deign to fulfill Thy high purposes in me whatever they be.
Work in and through me.
I am born to serve Thee, to be Thine, to be Thy instrument.
I ask not to see; I ask not to know,
I ask simply to be used.

He leads me where the waters glide, 117
The waters soft and still,
And homeward He will gently guide
My wandering heart and will.

Grant us, O Lord, to know that which is worth knowing, 118
to love that which is worth loving,
to praise what can bear with praise,
to hate what in thy sight is unworthy,
to prize what to thee is previous;
and above all to search out and do what is well-pleasing
unto thee, through Christ our Lord.

I come to you with thanksgiving. You have fortified me on every side 175
by providing for my needs. Speak to me now and help me to understand what you want of me. Fill my conversation with wisdom, and my silence with holy thoughts. Guide me with the Holy Spirit that I may bless you always for what you have done.

GUIDANCE

My guardian angel, 8
I honor and love you as my special friend.
Be with me at my side to guard me and care for me,
and to guide me as I go about my life this day.

I ask thee, Blessed Jesus, for thy blessing and thy guidance as I face the 175
tasks of life. Help me to always aim high in my ambitions and to enlarge
my vision of the possibilities for growth, for love, and for service to others.
Show me each day how to make my good intentions turn into benefits for
those I encounter. Let my light shine always with a kindly glow.

Guide me, O Lord, in all the changes and varieties of the world; that in 199
all things that shall happen, I may have an evenness and tranquility
of spirit; that my soul may be wholly resigned to Thy divinest will and
pleasure, never murmuring at Thy gentle chastisements and fatherly
correction.

Be quiet, soul: 8
Why shouldst thou care and sadness borrow,
Why sit in nameless fear and sorrow,
The live-long day?
God will make out thy path tomorrow
In his best way.

Given the hardest terms, supposing our days are indeed but a shadow, 166
even so, we may well adorn and beautify, in scrupulous self-respect, our
souls and whatever our souls touch upon.

HAPPINESS

***

Happiness does not come from getting what we want, but in wanting what we get. Like the song, if you can't be near the one you love, then love the one you're near. Maybe it all comes from loving freely without expectations.

***

Lord, with what courage and delight 205
I do each thing,
When Thy least breath sustains my wing! I shine and move
Like those above,
And, with much gladness
Quitting sadness,
Make me fair days of every night.

Live while you live, life calls for all your powers; 105
This instant day your utmost strength demands.
He wastes himself who stops to watch the sands
And, miser-like, hoards up the golden hours.

Happiness grows at our own firesides, and is not to be picked up in stranger's gardens. 114

Be good yourself and the world will be good. 170-C

The happiness of life is made up of minute fractions-the little soon forgotten charities of a kiss or smile, a kind look, a heartfelt compliment, and the countless infinitesimals of pleasurable and genial feelings. 42

Little drops of water, 37
Little grains of sand,
Make the mighty ocean
And the pleasant land.

Little deeds of kindness,
Little words of love,
Make our world an Eden
Like the Heaven above.

Happiness is everywhere, and its spring is in our own heart. 180

It's no in books, it's no in learn, 32
To make us truly blest;
If happiness has not her seat
And centre in the breast,
We may be wise, or rich, or great,
But never can be blest.

You traverse the world in search of happiness, which is within the reach of every man; a contented mind confers it on all. 102

HAPPINESS

Let not another's disobedience to Nature become an ill to you, 64
For you were not born to be depressed and unhappy with others, but to be happy with them.
And if any is unhappy, remember that he is so for himself; for God made all men to enjoy felicity and peace.

Where your pleasure is, there is your treasure: where your treasure, 181-A-6
there your heart: where your heart, there your happiness.

We can't choose happiness, either for ourselves or for another; we can't 60
tell where that will lie. We can only choose whether we will indulge ourselves in the present moment, or whether we will renounce that for the sake of being true to all the motives that sanctify our lives. I know this belief is hard; it has slipped away from me again and again; but I have felt that if I let it go forever, I should have no light through the darkness of this life.

It is not so much by what we attain in this life that we are to be made 16
happy, as by the enlivening hope of what we shall reach in the world to come. While a man is stringing a harp, he tries the strings, not for music, but for construction. When it is finished it shall be played for melodies. God is fashioning the human heart for future joy. He only sounds a string here and there to see how far his work has progressed.

HEALING and HEALTH

****

Just as we shouldn't expect miracles if we have no faith in them, we cannot have health without taking care of our minds and bodies by following common sense rules of diet, exercise, and an even temperament. Health is the most valuable of all possessions. If you have it, guard it well.

****

Refuse to be ill. Never tell people you are ill; never own it to yourself. 29
Illness is one of those things which a man should resist on principle at the onset.

A sound mind in a sound body is a short but full description of a happy 132
state in this world: he that has these two has little more to wish for, and he that wants either of them will be but little the better for anything else.

Dear God, help me to form good habits which will protect both my mind 175
and body from the darkness of sickness. Let me exercise sensibly and eat only wholesome foods so that I do not cause myself suffering. Charge my soul with joy, my mind with power, and my body with vitality so that I may serve Thee well.

Merciful God, I appeal to Thee, I beg humbly and from my heart, take 175
me into thy care. Fold me in your arms, and ward off my fears, soothe my pains, and guard me against the despair which threatens my spirit. Show me the path I need to take to effect a return to well being. Comfort me in my affliction, succor me in my distress, remain with me, strengthen me, and bless me with a return to health.

Blessed Mother, through thy intercession, bless those who are sick, infirm, 175
injured, or suffering. Ease their pain and torment, heal the wounds, and mend the hurt. Let them see the light of love, the joy of understanding, and the peace of serenity in the knowledge of thy care.

GRATITUDE FOR HEALTH 175

I come to thank The, O Lord, for the blessing of good health which has been given unto me. I awake each morning with a grateful heart for my body is without pain, my mind is clear, my spirit is tranquil, and my soul is filled with love of life and of you. Keep me ever close with Thy care.

GRATITUDE FOR RESTORED HEALTH 175

O God, I now appear before thy most holy face, and thank thee from my innermost soul, because thou hast raised me from my sickbed. My plea was heard and I was given the strength to overcome my affliction. Thy mercy has brought me to my feet and better health. Help me to use my recovery for good, for in my sickness I have learned that worldly goods have the value of dust. Let me use my recovery as a gift from God, and share my gratitude with love for others and assistance to anyone who needs my caring.

HOLIDAYS – SPECIAL DAYS

****

Special days give one a chance to do special things Write that long delayed letter which should be answered, call someone you haven't heard from in a year or more, indulge yourself with a small pleasure you don't usually have time for, or spend the day in bed with a good book. Do what you wan. You deserve it.

****

NEW YEAR'S GIFT 59

'Tis custom, Lord, this day to send
A gift to every common friend,
And shall I find no gift for Thee,
That art the best of friends to me?
There's nothing which my thoughts survey
My life, my soul, the light, the day -
But they are all Thy gifts to me.
And shall I find no gift for Thee?
Yea, Lord, behold I now confer
My life, my soul, and whatso'er
Thy liberal hand hath given me
Back as a New Year's gift to Thee.

FOR MOTHER'S DAY 8

Lord, I thank thee for the blessing I was given in having a loving mother. Let her example guide me on my journey through life's trials. Help me keep in mind that her faults were so small when compared to the virtues she practiced in her life and those high ideals of character which she impressed upon the mind of my youth. May I keep her caring always close as a reminder of unselfish love and devotion.

CHRISTMAS 211

Blow, bugles of battle, the marches of peace;
East, west, north, and south let the long quarrel cease.
Sing the song of great joy that the angels began.
Sing the glory of God and of goodwill to man!

NEW YEAR'S PRAYER 8

This day we pray, may my lips speak only truth. May my heart be pure, my spirit right. May faults be eliminated. May my activities be wholesome. May my tongue refrain from all criticism. May my body be healthy, my mind clear, and my faith increased day by day.

ON GOOD FRIDAY 122

O Christ, give us patience, and faith,
and hope as we kneel at the foot of Thy Cross, and hold fast to it.
Teach us by Thy Cross, that however ill the world may go,
the Father so loved us that He spared not Thee.

HOPE

****

Despite discouragement, desertion, disappointments, or disaster, we must cling to hope for better times if we are to survive and prosper.

****

Walk on a rainbow trail; walk on a trail of song. 156
And all about you will be beauty.
There is a way out of every dark mist, over a rainbow trail.

The word which God has written on the brow of every man is Hope. 106

Hope, like a gleaming taper's light, 82
Adorns and cheers our way;
And still, as darker grows the night,
Emits a brighter ray.

O Lord, in whom is our hope; remove far from us, 178
we pray Thee, empty hopes and presumptuous confidence.
Make our hearts so right with Thy most holy and loving heart,
that hoping in Thee we may do good;
until that day when faith and hope shall be abolished by sight and possession, and love shall be all in all.

Hope is itself a species of happiness, and, perhaps, the chief happiness 115
which this world affords.

Discouraged in the work of life, 134
Disheartened by its load,
Shamed by its failure or its fears,
I sink beside the road;
But let me only think of Thee,
And then new heart springs up in me.

It would appear that our nature is not, for any length of time, capable 81
of perfect resignation. Hope will make its way into the mind, and with hope, activity, and with activity, the realization of hope.

Know, then, whatever cheerful and serene 11
Supports the mind supports the body too.
Hence the most vital movement mortals feel
Is hope: the balm and life-biood of the soul.

Hope is the better half of courage. Hope! Has it not sustained the work 14
and given the fainting heart time and patience to outwit the chances and changes of life.

Auspicious hope! In thy sweet garden grow 35
Wreaths for each toil, a charm for every woe.

HUMILITY

****

Proverbs 22:4 tells us that "By humility and the fear of Lord are riches, and honor, and life."

****

It is no great thing to be humble when you are brought low; but to be humble when you are praised is a great and rare attainment. 181-B-4

Lord! Subdue our selfish will; 210
Each to each our tempers suit,
By Thy modulating skill,
Heart to heart, as lute to lute.

I have three precious things, which I hold fast and prize. The first is gentleness; the second is frugality; the third is humility, which keeps me from putting myself before others. Be gentle and you can be bold; be frugal, and you can be liberal; avoid putting yourself before others, and you can become a leader among men. 125

O love that passeth knowledge, come into my heart with all Thy fullness, that my heart may be made gentle with Thy gentleness. Grant me to bear other's burdens that I may cease to live for myself. Come Thou in that I may cease to be my own. Let me share with Thee in the bearing of the sin and sorrow of the vast world; let me take up the crosses of the laboring and the heavy-laden. Fill me with thyself that I may become the servant of humanity. 146

Grant, I pray, O Lord, that with that lowliness of mind that befits my humble condition, and that elevation of soul which Thy majesty demands, I may ever adore Thee; in that hope which Thy clemency permits. May I submit myself to Thee as all-powerful, leave myself in Thy hand, as all-wise, and turn unto Thee as all-perfect and good. I beseech Thee, most merciful Father, that Thy most vivid fire may purify me, that Thy clearest light may illuminate me, and that purest love of Thine may so advance me that, held back by no mortal influence, I may return safe and happy to Thee. 43

It is in vain to gather virtues with humility; for the spirit of God delights to dwell in the hearts of the humble. 181-E-1

O God, Who through Thy Son Jesus Christ hast promised a blessing to the meek upon the earth, take from us all pride and vanity, boasting and forwardness, and give us the true courage that shows itself by gentleness, the true wisdom that shows itself by simplicity, and the true power that shows itself by modesty. 122

Blessed be thy name. Protect me from vanity and deceit, for I know it is only in humility that I can hope for security. I know that in building my spiritual house, your blessing will be upon me today and always. Let me be an instrument in bringing joy to others for that is surely the way my soul will be made joyous. 175

HUMILITY

Hear our prayers, O Lord, and consider our desires. 199
Give unto us true humility, a meek and quiet spirit,
a loving and a friendly heart, a holy and a useful manner of life;
bearing the burdens of our neighbors, denying ourselves,
and studying to benefit others, and to please Thee in all things.
Grant us to be righteous in performing promises,
loving to our relatives, careful of our charges,
to be gentle and easy to be entreated, slow to anger,
and readily prepared for every good work.

Teach thy tongue to say, "I do not know." 20-G

He that is down, needs fear no fall; 30
He that is low, no pride;
He that is humble ever shall
Have God to be his guide.

Do not consider yourself to have made any spiritual progress, unless 118
you account yourself the least of all men. God walks with the humble; he reveals himself to the lowly; he gives understanding to the little ones; he discloses his meaning to pure minds, but hides his grace from the curious and the proud.

If thou desire the love of God and man, be humble, for the proud heart, 172
as it loves none but itself, is beloved of none but itself. Humility enforces where neither virtue, nor strength, nor reason can prevail.

Humble we must be, if to Heaven we go; 98
High is the root there; but the gate is low:
When e'er thou speak'st, look with a lowly eye:
Grace is increased by humility.

Humility is the genuine proof of Christian virtue. Without it we keep all 126
our defects; and they are only crusted over by pride, which conceals them from others, and often from ourselves.

Should you ask me: What is the first thing in religion? I should reply: 181-A-6
The first, second, and third thing therein is humility.

IMMORTALITY

****

True, there is no proof of life after death ... but neither is there any evidence that there isn't a new beginning after it either.

****

We sometimes congratulate ourselves at the moment of waking from a 91
troubled dream: it may be so the moment after death.

They that love beyond the world cannot be separated by it. Death cannot 167
kill what never dies, nor can spirits ever be divided that love and live in the
same divine principle .... Death is but crossing the world, as friends do the
seas; they live in one another still.

Our Creator would never have made such lovely days, and have given us 91
the deep hearts to enjoy them, above and beyond all thought, unless we
were meant to be immortal.

I am fully convinced that the soul is indestructible, and that its activities 81
will continue through eternity. It is like the sun, which, to our eyes, seems
to set at night; but it has really gone to diffuse its light elsewhere.

> To love abundantly is to live abundantly, 8
> and to love forever is to live forever.

> Oh, may I join the choir invisible 60
> Of those immortal dead who live again
> In minds made better by their presence; live
> In pulses stirred to generosity,
> In deeds of rectitude, in scorn
> For miserable aims that end with self,
> In thoughts sublime that pierces the night like stars,
> And with their mild persistence urge men's search
> To vaster issues.

Being us, O Lord God, at the last awakening into the house and gate of 54
heaven, to enter into that gate and dwell in that house, where there shall
be no darkness nor dazzling, but one equal light; no noise nor silence, but
one equal music, no fear nor hopes, but an equal possession; no ends nor
beginnings, but one equal eternity; in the habitations of Thy Majesty and
Thy Glory, world without end.

Our Lord has written the promise of the resurrection, not in books 137
alone, but in every leaf in springtime.

> This life is but the passage of a day, 178
> This life is but a pang and all is over:
> But in the life to come which fades not away
> Every love shall abide and every lover.

IMMORTALITY

Out of the dusk a shadow, 197
Then a spark;
Out of the cloud a silence,
Then, a lark;
Out of the heart a rapture,
Then, a pain;
Out of the dead, cold ashes,
Life again.

To live in hearts we leave behind 35
Is not to die.

If I err in my belief that the souls of men are immortal, I err gladly, nor 40
do I wish this error, in which I find delight, to be wrested from me.

Were a star quenched on high, 133
For ages would its light,
Still traveling downward from the sky,
Shine on our mortal sight.
So when a great man dies,
For years beyond our ken,
The light he leaves behind him lies
Upon the paths of men.

He is not dead, this friend; not dead, 195
But, in the path we mortals tread,
Got some few, trifling steps ahead,
And nearer to the end;
So that you, too, once past the bend
Shall meet again, as face to face this friend
You fancy dead.

I feel my immortality o'ersweep all pains, all tears, all time, all fears; 33
and peal, like the eternal thunders of the deep, into my ears this truth
--thou livest forever!

Can it be? Matter immortal? And shall spirit die? Above the nobler, shall 217
less nobler rise? Shall man alone, for whom all else revives, no resurrection
know? Shall man alone, imperial man! Be sown in barren ground less
privileged than grain, on which he feeds?

This life is only a prelude to eternity. For that which we call death is 185
but a pause, in truth a progress into life.

JUSTICE

****

If justice means receiving what one is entitled to receive, then it follows that we must deal with others in a fair and just manner.

****

The deeds we do, the words we say, 117
Into still air they seem to fleet,
We count them ever past;
But they shall last, -
In the dread judgment they
And we shall meet.

Judge not, and ye shall not be judged; condemn not, and ye shall not 20-A
be condemned; forgive, and ye shall be forgiven.

Let wickedness escape, as it may at the bar, it never fails of doing justice 185
upon itself; for every guilty person is his own hangman.

Though the mills of God grind slowly, yet they grind exceeding small. 133

Man is unjust, but God is just; and finally justice triumphs. 133

Foolish men imagine that because judgment for an evil thing is delayed, 36
there is no justice, but only accident here below. Judgment for an evil thing is many times delayed some day or two, some century or two, but it is sure as life, it is sure as death!

Deal with another as you'd have 20-D
Another deal with you;
What you're unwilling to receive,
Be sure you never do.

Almighty God, beseech thy advocacy on my behalf. Give to those 8
who judge the spirit of wisdom and understanding that they may discern the truth. Allow them to render justice moderated with compassion and mercy.

His gain is loss: 200
For he that wrongs his friends
Wrongs himself more,
And ever has about him a silent court and jury
And he, the prisoner at the bar ever condemned.

O Glorious Saint Basil, grant me thy strength and protection. Make that 175
which is evil good, and preserve the just in their righteousness. For thou can do all things and will surely save those who are worthy from oppression and injustice. For those who desire liberation, thou will set free. Bless me this day, I pray.

Heaven gives long life to the just and the intelligent. 45

JUSTICE

What will be the punishment? Perhaps nothing else than, not having 64
none thy duty, thou wilt lose the character of fidelity, modesty, propriety.
Do not look for greater penalties than these.

Thou art indeed just, Lord, if I contend 101
With thee; but, sir, so what I plead is just.
Why do sinners' ways prosper? And why must
Disappointment all I endeavor end?

Whoever fights, whoever falls, 63
Justice conquers, evermore...
And he who battles on her side,
God, though he were ten times slain,
Crowns him victor glorified,
Victor over death and pain.

God's justice is a bed where we 68
Our anxious hearts may lay
And, weary with ourselves, may sleep
Our discontent away.
For right is right, since God is God;
And right the day must win;
To doubt would be disloyalty,
To falter would be sin.

Man judges from a partial view. 211
None ever yet his brother knew;
The Eternal Eye that sees the whole
May better read the darkened soul,
And find, to outward sense denied,
The flower upon its inmost side!

An honest man nearly always thinks justly. 179

God's justice, tardy though it prove perchance 26
Rests never on the track until it reach
Delinquency.

Justice and power must be brought together, so that whatever is just 165
may be powerful, and whatever is powerful may be just.

KINDNESS

****

Kindness... to be pleasant, gentle, generous, sympathetic. Practice it often daily so that it becomes a habit.

****

"What is real good?" 161
I asked in musing mood.
Order, said the law court;
Knowledge, said the school;
Truth, said the wise man;
Pleasure, said the fool;
Love, said a maiden;
Beauty, said the page;
Freedom, said the dreamer;
Home, said the sage;
Fame, said the soldier;
Equity, the seer;-
Spake my heart full sadly,
"The answer is not here."
Then within my bosom
Softly this I heard:
"Each heart holds the secret;
Kindness is the word."

Kind words are the music of the world. They have a power which seems 68
to be beyond natural causes, as if they were some angel's song which had
lost its way and comes on earth. It seems as if they could do what in reality
God alone can do—soften the hard and angry hearts of men. No one was
ever corrected by sarcasm—crushed, perhaps, if the sarcasm was clever
enough, but drawn nearer to God, never.

God is merciful to those who are kind. 170-F

So many gods, so many creeds, 213
So many roads that wind and wind,
And yet the art of being kind
Is all this sad world needs.

Whoever gives a small coin to a poor man has six blessings bestowed 20-G
upon him, but he who speaks a kind word to him obtains eleven blessings.

'Twas a thief said the last kind word to Christ: 26
Christ took the kindness and forgave the theft.

A smile on your lips; 8
Cheers your heart,
Keeps you in good humor,
Preserves peace in your soul,
Promotes your health,
Beautifies your face
Induces kindly thoughts,
Inspires kindly deeds.

LIFE

****

An anonymous bit goes like this. "There may be a Heaven, there must be a Hell; Meanwhile, we have our life here—Well?"

****

Be not afraid of life. Believe that life is worth living and your beliefs will 112
help create the fact.

Life is like unto a long journey with a heavy load. Let thy step be slow 74-B
and steady, that thou stumble not.
Persuade thyself that imperfections and inconveniences are the natural law of mortals, and there will be no room for discontent, neither for despair.
When ambitious desires arise in thy heart, recall the days of extremity thou has passed through.
If thou knowest only what it is to conquer, and know not what it is to be defeated, woe unto thee - it will fare ill with thee.
Look upon wrath as thine enemy.
Find fault with thyself rather than with others.
Better the less than the more.

LIFE 33

Well - well, the world must turn upon its axis,
And all mankind turn with it, heads or tails,
And live and die, make love and pay our taxes,
And as the veering wind shifts, shifts our sails;
The kind commands us and the doctor quacks us,
The priest instructs, and so our life exhales;
A little breath, love, wine, ambition, fame,
Fighting, devotion, dust, - perhaps a name.

LIVE NOW 102

Let hope and sorrow, fear and anger be,
And think each day that dawns the last you'll see;
For so the hour that greets you unforeseen
Will bring with it enjoyment twice as keen.

QUESTION 175

You live
To eat and sleep and drink
And walk and speak and see
I live
To laugh and love and dream
And sing and dance and weep.
We die. And who knows whether
You or I lived life better?

Life can only be understood backward, but it must be lived forward. 121

LIFE

Learn to live well, or fairly make your will; 169
You've played, and loved, and ate, and drank your fill:
Walk sober off, before a sprightlier age
Comes tittering on, and shoves you from the stage.

PRAYER FOR A HOLY LIFE 181-T-3

Merciful God, grant that I may ardently desire, carefully search out and truthfully acknowledge and perfectly fulfill all things that are pleasing to you. Grant, O Lord, that I may not fail you in times of joy or sadness. May I be neither proud in my success nor discouraged by my failure? Let me rejoice only in what leads to you and sorrow over only that which takes me away from you. Lord, let me be obedient without resentment, poor without meanness, chaste without pride, patient without hesitation, humble without deceit, joyful without being silly, serious without heaviness, and in all things ready to please you.

God asks no man whether he will accept life. 16
That is not the choice. You must take it.
The only choice is how.

Be such a man, and live such a life, 24
That if every man were such as you,
And every life a life like yours,
This earth would be God's Paradise.

He lives long that lives well; and time misspent is not lived, but lost. 76
God is better than his promise if he takes from him a long lease, and gives him a freehold of a better value.

We are in this life as it were in another man's house.... In heaven is 79
our home, in the world is our Inn: do not so entertain thyself in the Inn of this world for a day as to have thy mind withdrawn from longing after thy heavenly home.

But helpless Pieces of the Game He plays 160
Upon this Checker-board of Nights and Days;
Hither and thither moves, and checks, and slays,
And one by one back in the Closet lays.

LOVE

****

Love—a simple answer to all life's complex problems. Try it—it works!

****

I hold it true, whatever befall; 200
I feel it when I sorrow most;
'Tis better to have loved and lost
Than never to have loved at all.

Love, indeed, is the source of all good things; it is an impregnable 181-F-3
defense, and the way that leads to heaven. He who walks in love can neither go astray nor be afraid; love guides him, protects him, and brings him to his journey's end.

Love! Thou hast every bliss in store: 77
'Tis friendship and 'tis something more;
Each other every wish they give:
Not to know love is not to live.

Love and you shall be loved. All love is mathematically just, as much 63
as the two sides of an algebraic equation.

Trials must and will befall; 48
But with humble faith to see
Love inscribed upon them all,
This is happiness to me.

If you would be loved, love and be lovable. 73

Love is the master key that opens the gates of happiness. 100

In peace, Love tunes the shepherd's reed; 184
In war, he mounts the warrior's steed:
In halls, in gay attire is seen;
In hamlets, dances on the green;
Love rules the court, the camp, the grove,
And men below, and saints above;
For love is heaven and heaven is love.

The true measure of loving God is to love him without measure. 181-B-4

FOR LOVE'S GROWTH 181-A-6
Grant me, even me, my dearest Lord, to know Thee, and love Thee, and rejoice in Thee. And, if I cannot do these perfectly in this life, let me at least advance to higher degrees every day. Till I can come to do them in perfection, let the knowledge of Thee increase in me here, that it may be full hereafter. Let the love of Thee grow every day more and more here. That it may be perfect hereafter; that my joy may be great in it, and full in Thee. I know, O God that Thou art a God of truth, O make well Thy gracious promises to me, that my joy may be full.

LOVE

ADORATION 84

I love my God, but with no love of mine,
For I have none to give;
I love thee, Lord, but all that love is Thine
For by thy life I live.
I am as nothing, and rejoice to be
Emptied and lost and swallowed up in thee.

Thou Lord, alone, art all thy children need
And there is none beside;
From thee the streams of blessedness proceed;
In thee the blest abide,
Fountain of life and all-abounding grace,
Our source, our center and our dwelling place!

Love is never lost. If not reciprocated it will flow back and soften and 110
purify the heart.

Kindle my coldness with the fire of Thy love, 118
and enlighten my blindness with the brightness of Thy presence.

There is no happiness in the world in which love does not enter; and 189
love is but the discovery of ourselves in others, and the delight in the recognition.

A BIT OF ADVICE 58

If ye would love and loved be,
In mind keep well these things three,
And sadly in thy breast imprint,
Be secret, true and patient.

O Love, Love! Give me, O Lord, so strong a voice that when I
50
call Thee Love, I shall be heard from East to West, and in all parts of the world and in the depths of Hell, so that Thou mayest be known and adored as the True Love. O love, Thou suffusest and piercest, Thou bindest and yet loosest, Thou art ruler over all. O Love, Thou art heaven and earth, air and fire, blood and water: Thou art man and God!
O Love, who are neither known nor loved,
Love, give thyself to all Thy creatures!
Love, who canst not find a place in which to rest, come Thou into my being.
O Souls, created by love for Love, why dost Thou fail to love Love?
And what is Love except God?
O Love, that causeth me to be consumed, Thou makest me to die even though I live!
O Souls, be in love with Love,
Come forth to love,
O Souls, come forth to love Love!

LOVE

The supreme happiness of life is the conviction of being loved for your- 106
self, or, more correctly, being loved in spite of yourself.

Love all God's creation, the whole and every grain of sand in it. 55
Love every leaf, every ray of God's light.
Love the animals, love the plants, and love everything.
If you love everything, you will perceive the divine mystery in things.
Once you perceive it, you will begin to comprehend it better every day.
And you will come at last to love the whole world with an all-embracing love.

Do right, and God's recompense to you will be the power of doing 176
more right. Give, and God's reward to you will be the spirit of giving
more; a blessed spirit, for it is the Spirit of God himself, whose Life is the
blessedness of giving. Love and God will pay you with the capacity of more
love; for love is Heaven—love is God within you.

Love is love for as long as it lasts, 175
But it's infatuation after it's past.

Grant, O Lord, my earnest plea. Help me to be kind and thoughtful in 175
word and deed. Help me to forget myself and draw love and affection
from those around me. Increase my force of body and mind to make me
inviting to those I find appealing. I am most thankful for the love of others
which thou have put into my own heart. Lead me in this search, I ask most
humbly.

FOR A DREAM TO SEE A FUTURE HUSBAND 8

Sweet St. Lucy, let me know
Whose cloth I shall lay,
Whose bed I shall make,
Whose child I shall bear,
Whose darling I shall be,
Whose arms I shall lay in.

TO FIND A LOVER 175

Blessed St. Valentine, I come to you with a heart full of love yearning
to share its fullness with another. Help me find this person to share
my life which I pledge to fill with understanding, courtesy, fidelity, and
temperance. Let the law of kindness rule my life and govern all I say and
do. Be with me on my search, Blessed Valentine, and guide my way to one
who will care for me as I will care for my life's partner.

TO GET A HUSBAND 8

Sweet St. Catherine, send me a husband,
A good one, I pray,
But anyone better than none.
Oh, St. Catherine, lend me thine aid.
That I may not die an old maid.

LOVE

THE TREASURES OF LAO TZU 20-H

I have Three Treasures.
Guard them and keep them safe.
The first is Love.
The second is Moderation. The third is,
Never be the first in the world.
Having Love, one will be courageous.
Through Moderation, one has power to spare.
Through not presuming to be the first in the world,
One can develop one's talent and let it mature.
If one forsakes love and courage,
Forsakes restraint and reserve power,
Forsakes following behind and rushes in front,
He is doomed!
For love is victorious in attack and secure in defense.
Heaven arms with love those it would not see destroyed.

Fountain of love, love Thou our friends and teach them to love Thee with all their hearts, that they may think and speak and do only such things as are well-pleasing to Thee. 181-A-3

O Lord, grant us to love Thee; 155
Grant that we may love those that love Thee;
Grant that we may do the deeds that win Thy love.
Make the love of Thee to be dearer to us
Than ourselves and our families,
Than wealth, and even then cool water.

BITTER-SWEET 97

Ah, my dear angry Lord,
Since Thou dost love, yet strike;
Cast down, yet help afford;
Sure I will do the like.

I will complain, yet praise,
I will bewail, approve;
And all my sour sweet days
I will lament, and love.

Luke warmness I account a sin, 47
As great in love as in religion.

Yes, love indeed is light from heaven; 33
A spark of what Immortal fire
With angels shared by Allah given,
To life from earth our low desire.

SINCE THOU HAST GIVEN ME THIS GOOD HOPE, O GOD 195

Since thou hast given me this good hope, O God,
That while my footsteps tread the flowery sod
And the great woods embower me, and white dawn
And purple even sweetly lead me on
From day to day and night to night, O God,
My life shall no wise miss the light of love,
But ever climbing, climb above
Man's one poor star, man's supine lands,
Into the azure steadfastness of death.
My life shall no wise lack the light of love,
My hands not lack the loving touch of hands,
But day by day, while yet I draw my breath,
And day by day unto my last of years,
I shall be one that has a perfect friend,
Here heart shall taste my laughter and my tears,
And her kind eyes shall lead me to the end.

Love is not a possession but a growth. The heart is a lamp with just oil 16
enough to burn for an hour, and if there be no oil to put in again its light will go out. God's grace is the oil that fills the lamp of love.

The pains of love be sweeter far 57
Than all other pleasures are.

Life is short and we have never too much time for gladdening the hearts 6
of those who are traveling the dark way with us. Oh, be swift to love! Make haste to be kind!

We ought to love our Maker for His own sake, without either hope of 39
good or fear of pain.

MERCY

****

For those of us with good intentions... for those of us who are well acquainted with sin... for those of us who falter... do not despair, there is always mercy for those who ask God for it.

****

LORD! WHO ARE MERCIFUL AS WELL AS JUST 191

Lord! Who are merciful as well as just,
Incline Thine ear to me, a child of dust:
Not what I would, a Lord! I offer thee,
Alas! But what I can.
Father Almighty, who hast made me man,
And bade me look to heaven, for thou art there,
Accept my sacrifice and humble prayer.
Four things which are not in thy treasury,
I lay before thee, Lord, with this petition:
My nothingness, my wants,
My sins, my contrition.

Be merciful unto me, O God, be merciful, unto me: 20-A
for my soul trusteth in Thee; yea, in the shadow of Thy wings
will I make my refuge, until these calamities be over past.

The quality of mercy is not strained; 186
It droppeth, as the gentle rain from heaven
Upon the place beneath: it is twice blessed;
It blesseth him that gives, and him that takes.

Among the attributes of God, although they are all equal, mercy shines with even more brilliancy than justice. 39

Teach me to feel another's woe, 169
To hide the fault I see;
That mercy I to others show,
That mercy show to me.

GOD 68

Have mercy on us, God most high!
Who lift our hearts to Thee,
Have mercy on us worms of earth,
Most holy Trinity!

Most ancient of all mysteries!
Before Thy throne we lie;
Have mercy now, most merciful,
Most holy Trinity!

We hand folks over to God's mercy, and show none ourselves. 60

FOR MERCY 178
Before the beginning Thou hast foreknown the end,
Before the birthday the death-bed was seen of Thee.
Cleanse what I cannot cleanse; mend what I cannot mend,
O Lord, All-Merciful, be merciful to me.
While the end is drawing near I know not mine end;
Birth I recall not, my death I cannot foresee:
O God, arise to defend, arise to befriend,
O Lord All-Merciful, be merciful to me.

HAVE MERCY ON ME, O GOD 20-A

> Have mercy on me, O God, according to thy great mercy.
> And according to the multitude of thy tender mercies blot out my iniquity.
> Wash me yet more from my iniquity, and cleanse me from my sin.
> For I know my iniquity, and my sin is always before me...
> Turn away thy face from my sins, and blot out all my iniquities
> Create a clean heart in me, O God: and renew a right spirit within my bowels.
> Cast me not away from thy face; and take not thy holy spirit from me.
> Restore unto me the joy of thy salvation, and strengthen me with a perfect spirit.

He that has tasted the bitterness of sin fears to commit it; and he that hath felt the sweetness of mercy will fear to offend it. 48
Mercy to him that shows it; it is the rule.

O Lord, who art our Guide even unto death, grant us, I pray Thee, grace to follow Thee whithersoever Thou goest. In little daily duties to which Thou callest us, bow down our wills to simple obedience, patience under pain of provocation, strict truthfulness of word and manner, humility, kindness; in great acts of duty or perfection, if Thou shouldest call us to them, uplift us to self-sacrifice, heroic courage, laying down of life for Thy truth's sake, or for a brother. 178

O Lord, who art as the Shadow of a great Rock in a weary land, who beholdest Thy weak creatures weary of labor, weary of pleasure, weary of hope deferred, weary of self; in Thine abundant compassion, and unutterable tenderness, bring us, I pray Thee, unto Thy rest. 178

MISCELLANEOUS

****

If, after having read this book through, you have not found a suitable thought for your special situation, write to the author and a sheet of helpful hints and inspiration will be sent to you.

****

IN ANY EMERGENCY 8

I call upon thee, St. Expeditus, in my day of trouble with confidence that you will be my help and my strength. Bring to me justice if my cause is just, triumph in my battle if my struggle is right, and hasty assistance as my need is urgent. Be my light in the darkness and my guide toward the pathway which will turn my enemies away from me so that I may live in peace, in love, and in praise of God.

FOR THE UNITED STATES 207

Almighty God; we make our earnest prayer that Thou wilt keep the United States in Thy holy protection; that Thou wilt incline the hearts of the citizens to cultivate a spirit of subordination and obedience to government... And finally that Thou wilt most graciously be pleased to dispose us all to do justice, to love mercy and to demean ourselves with that charity, humility and pacific temper of mind that were the characteristics of the Divine Author of our blessed religion, and without a humble imitation of whose example in these things we can never hope to be a happy nation. Grant our supplication, we beseech Thee, through Jesus Christ our Lord.

FOR RICH AND POOR 181-B-2

O God that art the sole hope of the world,
The only refuge for unhappy men,
Abiding in the faithfulness of Heaven,
Give me a strong succor in this testing-place.
O King, protect Thy man from utter ruin,
Lest the weak flesh surrender to the tyrant,
Facing innumerable blows alone.
Remember I am dust and wind and shadow.
And life is fleeting as the flower of the grass.

Almighty Lord, obtain for me thy grace of never attaching my heart to 175
the fleeting goods of this life. My vanity and my greed serve nothing which will enrich my spiritual life. And I need thy help in keeping my sights set on the uplifting spiritual values of caring only for others. My needs will be met in the same measure with which I share with those whose needs are more urgent than my own.

FOR A NEW BEGINNING 181-B-1

O Lord our God, great, eternal, wonderful in glory who keepest covenant and promise for those that love Thee with their whole heart; we come before Thee in this our new beginning, begging Thee to cleanse us from our sins, and from every thought displeasing to Thy goodness, that with a pure heart and a clear mind we may venture confidently and fearlessly to pray unto Thee; through Jesus Christ our Lord.

FOR LIGHT AND KNOWLEDGE 204

O grant us light, that we may know
The wisdom Thou alone canst give;
That truth may guide whatever we do,
And virtue bless wherever we live.

O grant us light, that we may learn
How dead is life from Thee apart;
How sure is joy for all who turn
To Thee an undivided heart.

God grant that you neither shame nor be shamed. 20-G

What have I learnt wherever I've been? 171
From all I've heard, from all I've seen?
What know I more that is worth the knowing?
What have I done that's worth the doing?
What have I sought that I should shun?
What duties have I left undone?

God does not decree that a man should be good or evil. It is only fools and ignoramuses among Gentiles and Jews who maintain this nonsense. Any man born is free to become as righteous as Moses, as wicked as Jeroboam, a student or an ignoramus, kind or cruel, generous or niggardly. 142

FOR AN ALCOHOLIC 175

Gracious Saint Matthias, the helper of all who put their trust in thee, we pray for all those enslaved by intoxicants, and especially for (state name). Give this one the desire and the will to be free, and the grace to continue in the path toward abstinence. I ask thy help in confidence that you can bring freedom to those bound by the chains of addiction.

AGAINST IMPURE THOUGHTS 175

With trust and faith I beg thee, Blessed St. Martin, to defend me against impure and evil thoughts which may stain my soul and come between my desire for the true and complete satisfaction which is offered through perfect love. Rescue me from the mire lest I sink. Let not the deep swallow me up. Thy mercy is great, draw near to me and lift me up, I pray.

FOR DEDICATION 181-I-1

Teach us, Good Lord, to serve Thee as Thou deservest;
To give and not to count the cost;
To fight and not to heed the wounds;
To toil and not to seek for rest;
To labor and not to ask for any reward,
Save that of knowing that we do thy will;
Through Jesus Christ our Lord.

MISCELLANEOUS

FOR THE FUTURE 115

Almighty God, merciful Father, who has granted me such continuance of life, that I now see the beginning of another year, look with mercy upon me; as Thou grantest increase of years, grant increase of grace. Let me live to repent what I have done amiss, and so help me to regulate my future life, that I may obtain mercy when I appear before Thee, through the merits of Jesus Christ. Enable me, O Lord, to do my duty with a quiet mind; and take not from me Thy Holy Spirit, but protect and bless me, for the sake of Jesus Christ.

FOR UNION WITH GOD 181-A-3

O Lord our God, grant us grace to desire Thee with our whole heart, that so desiring, we may seek and find Thee; and so finding Thee we may love Thee; and loving Thee we may hate those sins from which Thou has redeemed us; for the sake of Jesus Christ.

FOR ASPIRATION 181-A-6

Thee, Most Merciful God, do I now invoke to descend into my soul, which Thou has prepared for Thy reception by the desire which Thou hast breathed into it. Ere ever I cried to Thee, Thou, Most Merciful, hadst called and sought me, that I might find Thee, Lord, and desire to love Thee. Even so I sought and found Thee, Lord, and desire to love Thee. Increase my desire, and grant me what I ask. See, I love Thee, but too little; strengthen my love. When my spirit aspires to Thee, and meditates on Thine unspeakable goodness, the burden of the flesh becomes less heavy, the tumult of thought is stilled, and the weight of mortality is less oppressive. Then fain would my soul find wings, that she might rise in tireless flight ever upwards to Thy glorious throne, and there be filled with the refreshing solace that belongs to the citizens of heaven.

FOR COOPERATION 181-A-6

O Lord, our Saviour, Who has warned us that Thou wilt require much of those to whom much is given; grant that we whose lot is cast in so goodly a heritage may strive together the more abundantly by prayer, by almsgiving, by fasting, and by every other appointed means, to extend to others what we so richly enjoy, and as we have entered into the labours of other men, so to labour that in their turn other men may enter into ours, to the fulfillment of Thy holy will, and our own everlasting salvation; through Jesus Christ our Lord.

Nothing will ever be attempted if all possible objections must be first overcome. 115

FOR REMOVING OBSTRUCTIONS IN THE THROAT 8

Place both hands loosely around the neck and pray, "Blessed Blaise, martyr and servant of Jesus Christ, commands thee to pass up or down, by the law of the all powerful, go down or come out."

MISCELLANEOUS

GOD 197

I see Thee in the distant blue;
But in the violet's dell of dew,
Behold, I breathe and touch Thee too.

What you think of yourself is much more important than what others think of you. 185

A PRAYER FOR AID 151

Oh, make me see Thee, Lord, where'er I go!
If mortal beauty sets my soul on fire,
That flame when near to Thine must needs expire,
And I with love of only Thee shall glow.
Dear Lord, Thy help I seek against this woe,
These torments that my spirit vexes and tire;
Thou only with new strength canst re-inspire
My will, my sense, my courage faint and low.
Thou gavest me on earth this soul divine;
And Thou within this body weak and frail
Didst prison it - how sadly there to live!
How can I make its lot less vile than mine?
Without Thee, Lord, all goodness seems to fail.
To alter fate is God's prerogative.

Give me, O Lord, a steadfast heart, which no unworthy affection may drag downwards; give me an unconquered heart, which no tribulation can wear out; give me an upright heart, which no unworthy purpose may tempt aside. 181-T-3
Bestow upon me also, O Lord my God, understanding to know Thee, diligence to seek Thee, wisdom to find Thee, and faithfulness that may finally embrace Thee.

LORD, SAVE US. WE PERISH 178

O Lord, see us, O Lord, find us
In Thy patient care;
Be Thy Love before, behind us,
Round us, everywhere:
Lest the god of this world blind us,
Lest he speak us fair,
Lest he forge a chain to bind us,
Lest he bait a snare.
Turn not from us, call to mind us,
Find, embrace us, bear;
Be Thy Love before, behind us,
Round us, everywhere.

Natural liberty is the gift of the beneficent Creator of the whole human race. 87

MISCELLANEOUS

O God the Father, good beyond all that is good, fair beyond all that 181-D-1
is fair, in whom is calmness, peace, and concord; do thou make up the dissensions which divide us from each other, and bring us back into a unity of love which may bear some likeness to thy divine nature. And as thou art above all things, make us one by the unanimity of a good mind; that through the embrace of charity and the bonds of affection, we may be spiritually one, as well in ourselves as in each other; through that peace of thine which maketh all things peaceful, and through the grace, mercy, and tenderness of thy Son, Jesus Christ.

A PRAYER 58

O Lord, the hard-won miles
Have worn my stumbling feet:
Oh, soothe me with thy smiles,
And make my life complete.

The thorns were thick and keen
Where'er I trembling trod;
The way was long between
My wounded feet and God.

Where healing waters flow
Do thou my footsteps lead.
My heart is aching so;
Thy gracious balm I need.

If all the misfortunes of mankind were cast into a public stock, in order 190
to be equally distributed among the whole species, those who now think themselves the most unhappy would prefer the share they are already possessed of, before that which would fall to them by such a division.

God is in all that liberates and lifts, 135
In all that humbles, sweetens, and consoles.

FOR SELF-CONFIDENCE 23

Great God, I ask Thee for no meaner pelf
Than that I may not disappoint myself;
That in my action I may soar as high
As I can now discern with this clear eye.
And next in value, which Thy kindness lends,
That I may greatly disappoint my friends,
Howe'er they think or hope that it may be,
They may not dream how Thou'st distinguished me.
That my weak hand may equal my firm faith,
And my life practice more than my tongue saith;
That my low conduct may not show,
Nor my relenting lines,
That I Thy purpose did not know,
Or overrated Thy designs.

MISCELLANEOUS

FOR ENLIGHTENMENT 115

Almighty God, our Heavenly Father, without whose help labour is useless, without whose light search is vane, invigorate my studies, and direct my inquires, that I may, by due diligence and right discernment, establish myself and others in Thy holy faith. Take not, O Lord, Thy Holy Spirit from me; let not evil thoughts have dominion in my mind. Let me not linger in ignorance, but enlighten and support me; for the sake of Jesus Christ our Lord.

FOR FULFILLMENT 181-J-3

Almighty God, Who hast given us grace at this time with one accord to make our common supplications unto thee; and dost promise that when two or three are gathered together in Thy Name, Thou will grant their requests; fulfill now, O Lord, the desires and petitions of Thy servants, as may be most expedient for them; granting us in this world knowledge of Thy Truth, and in the world to come life everlasting.

Music has been called the speech of angels; I will go further, and call it the speech of God Himself. 122

God sent his singers on earth 133
With songs of gladness and mirth
That they might touch the hearts of men
And bring them back to Heaven again.

I do the very best I know how; the very best I can; and I mean to keep on doing it to the end. If the end brings me out all right, what is said against me will not amount to anything. If the end brings me out all wrong, then a legion of angels swearing I was right will make no difference. 130

Be genuine and strenuous; earn for yourself, and look for grace from those in high places; from the powerful, favor; from the active and good, advancement; from the many, affection; from the individual, love. 81

When you do anything from a clear judgment that it ought to be done, never shun the being seen to do it, even though the world should make a wrong supposition about it; for, if you do not act right, shun the action itself; but, if you do, why are you afraid of those who censure you wrongly? 64

Friendship between mortals can be contracted on no other terms than that one must some time mourn for the other's death. 115

Blessed is the man who is too busy to worry in the daytime and too sleepy to worry at night. 8

MISCELLANEOUS

FOR RACIAL HARMONY 8

O God, who hast made man in Thine own likeness and who dost love all whom Thou hast made, suffer us not because of difference in race, color, or condition, to separate ourselves from others and thereby from Thee; but teach us the unity of Thy family and the universality of Thy love. As Thy Son our Saviour was born of a Hebrew mother and ministered first to His brethren of the House of Israel, but rejoiced in the faith of a Syro-Phoenician woman, and of a Roman soldier, and suffered His cross to be carried by a man of Africa; teach us, also, while loving and serving our own, to enter into the communion of the whole family; and forbid that, from pride or hardness of heart, we should despise any for whom Christ died, or injure any in whom He lives. And this we pray through Jesus Christ our Lord.

FOR RESTORATION 181-A-6

Oh God our Father, hear me, who am trembling in this darkness, and stretch forth Thy hand unto me; hold forth Thy light before me; recall me from my wanderings; and, Thou being my guide, may I be restored to myself and to Thee.

FOR THE FALSELY ACCUSED 178

O Lord, strengthen and support, we entreat Thee all persons unjustly accused or underrated. Comfort them by the ever present thought that Thou knowest the whole truth, and wilt, in Thine own good time, make their righteousness as clear as the light.
Give them grace to pray for such as do them wrong, and hear and bless them when they pray; for the sake of Jesus Christ our Lord and Savior.

FOR FAITHFULNESS 181-R-1

Thanks be to Thee, O Lord Jesus Christ, for all the benefits which Thou hast given us;
for all the pains and insults which Thou hast borne for us.
O Most Merciful Redeemer, Friend and Brother,
may we know Thee more clearly, love Thee more dearly,
and follow Thee more nearly day by day; for Thine own sake.

A SIOUX PRAYER 170-G

Grandfather, Great Spirit, you have been always, and before you nothing has been. There is no one to pray to but you. The star nations all over the heavens are yours, and yours are the grasses of the earth. You are older than all need, older than all pain and prayer.

Grandfather, Great Spirit, all over the world the faces of living ones are alike. With tenderness they have come up out of the ground. Look upon your children, with children in their arms, that they may face the winds and walk the good road to the day of quiet.

Grandfather, Great Spirit, fill us with the light. Give us the strength to understand and the eyes to see. Teach us to walk the soft earth as relatives to all that live. Help us, for without you we are nothing.

MISCELLANEOUS

FAILURE 8

Failure doesn't mean you are a failure...
    It does mean you haven't succeeded yet.
Failure doesn't mean you have accomplished nothing...
    It does mean you have learned something.
Failure doesn't mean you have been a fool...
    It does mean you had a lot of faith.
Failure doesn't mean you've been disgraced...
    It does mean you were willing to try.
Failure doesn't mean you can't have it...
    It does mean you have to do something in a different way.
Failure doesn't mean you are inferior...
    It does mean you are not perfect.
Failure doesn't mean you've wasted your life...
    It does mean you have a reason to start afresh.
Failure doesn't mean you should give up...
    It does mean you must try harder.
Failure doesn't mean you'll never make it...
    It does mean it will take a little longer.
Failure doesn't mean God has abandoned you...
    It does mean God has a better idea!

A PRAYER FOUND IN CHESTER CATHEDRAL 8

Give me a good digestion, Lord,
And also something to digest;
Give me a healthy body, Lord,
With sense to keep it at its best.

Give me a healthy mind, Lord,
To keep the good and pure in sight;
Which, seeing sin, is not appalled,
But finds a way to set it right.

Give me a mind that is not bored,
That does not whimper, whine or sigh;
Don't let me worry overmuch,
About the fussy thing called "I."

Give me a sense of humour, Lord;
Give me the grace to see a joke;
To get some happiness from life,
And pass it on to other folk.

GOD'S PLEDGE TO YOU 8

Not cloudless days; No rose-strewn ways;
Not care-free years, Devoid of sorrow's tears -
But—strength to bear—Your load of human care.
And grace to live aright—And keep your raiment white,
And love to see you through; That is God's pledge to you.

I would like the Angels of Heaven to be amongst us. 21
I would like the abundance of peace.
I would like full vessels of charity.
I would like rich treasures of mercy.
I would like cheerfulness to preside over all.
I would like Jesus to be present.
I would like the three Marys of illustrious renown to be with us.
I would like the friends of Heaven to be gathered around us from all parts.
I would like myself to be a rent-payer to the Lord; that I should suffer distress and that He would bestow a good blessing upon me.

FOR IMPROVEMENT 17
We must praise Thy goodness,
that Thou hast left nothing undone to draw us to Thyself.
But one thing we ask of Thee, our God,
not to ease Thy work in our improvement.
Let us tend towards Thee, no matter by what means,
and be fruitful in good works, for the sake of Jesus Christ our Lord.

Seldom can the heart be lonely, 89
    If it seeks a lonelier still;
Self-forgetting, seeking only
    Emptier cups of love to fill.

Never to tire, never to grow cold; 6
to be patient, sympathetic, tender;
to look for the budding flower and the opening heart;
to hope always;
like God, to love always - this is duty.

Everybody thinks of changing humanity and nobody thinks of changing themselves. 202

In the conduct of life, habits count for more than maxims; because habit is a living maxim, becomes flesh and instinct. To reform one's maxims is nothing: it is but to change the title of the book. To learn new habits is everything, for it is to reach the substance of life. Life is but a tissue of habits. 6

Since Thou Thyself dost still display 153
Unto the pure in heart,
Oh, make us children of the day
To know Thee as Thou art.
For Thou art light and life and love;
And Thy redeemed below
May see Thee as Thy saints above,
And know Thee as they know.

It is a misery to be born, a pain to live, a trouble to die. 181-B-4

MISCELLANEOUS

Govern all by thy wisdom, O Lord, so that my soul may always be 181-T-1
serving thee as thou dost will, and not as I may choose. Do not punish me,
I beseech thee, by granting that which I wish or ask, if it offends thy love,
which would always live in me. Let me die to myself, that so I may serve
thee: let me live to thee, who in thyself art the true Life.

Go put your creed into your deed, 63
Nor speak with double tongue.

Never esteem anything as of advantage to thee that shall make thee 12
break thy word or lose thy self-respect.

LORD OF ALL LIFE 100

Lord of all life, below, above,
Whose light is truth, whose warmth is love,
Before Thy ever-blazing throne
We ask no luster of our own.

Grant us Thy truth to make us free,
And kindling hearts that burn for Thee,
Till all Thy living altars claim
One holy light, one heavenly flame.

He who sacrifices his conscience to ambition burns a picture to obtain 170-A
the ashes.

We discover in ourselves what others hide from us, and we recognize 206
in others what we hide from ourselves.

Whoever has two loaves of bread, let him trade one for a narcissus; for 155
bread is nourishment for the body, but the narcissus in nourishment for
the soul.

Great minds have purposes, others have wishes. 110
Little minds are tamed and subdued by misfortune;
but great minds rise above it.

There are three marks of a superior man: 45
Being virtuous, he is free from anxiety;
Being wise, he is free from perplexity;
Being brave, he is free from fear.

God moves in a mysterious way 48
His wonders to perform;
He plants his footsteps in the sea,
And rides upon the storm.

This above all: to thine own self be true; 186
And it must follow, as the night the day,
Thou canst not then be false to any man.

NATURE and ANIMALS

****

I am always amazed at those who say they do not believe in God. Did man make a sunset, music in the breeze, a rose bud, a new-born baby, a moonlit beach, or a running brook?

****

Flower in the crannied wall, 200
I pluck you out of the crannies
I hold you here, root and all, in my hand,
Little flower—but if I could understand
What you are, root and all, and all in all,
I should know what God and man is.

If we do not find God in nature we may conclude, either that we do 139
not understand the expression of nature, or have mistaken ideas or poor feelings about him.

Never lose an opportunity of seeing anything that is beautiful; for 63
beauty is God's handwriting-a wayside sacrament. Welcome it in every fair face, in every fair sky, in every fair flower, and thank God for it as a cup of blessing.

JUDGE NOT ACCORDING TO THE APPEARANCE 178
Lord, purge our eyes to see
Within the seed a tree,
Within the glowing egg a bird,
Within the shroud a butterfly.

Till taught by such, we see
Beyond all creatures Thee,
And harken for Thy tender word,
And hear it, "Fear not: it is I."

Have pity, O Lord God, lest they who go by the way trample on the 181-A-6
unfledged bird, and send Thine angel to replace it in the nest, that it may live till it can fly.

What is lovely never dies, 5
But passes into other loveliness,
Stardust, or sea-foam, flower or winged air.

He prayeth well who loveth well 42
Both man and bird and beast.
He prayeth best who loveth best
All things, both great and small;
For the dear God who loveth us
He made and loveth all.

TO PROTECT CATTLE 8
Sprinkle the cattle with salt and holy water, and say over each one: "St. Thomas, preserve thee from all sickness."

PATIENCE

****

My personal prayer has always been, "God, give me patience, and I want it NOW."

****

Patience and fortitude conquer all things. 63

He who can endure all things may venture all things. 206

How poor are they who have not patience! 186
What wound did ever heal, but by degrees?

Patience is power; with time and patience the mulberry tree becomes silk. 170-A

What cannot be removed becomes lighter through patience. 102

The falling drops at last will wear the stones. 136

Be patient with everyone, but above all with yourself. 181-F-1
I mean, do not be disturbed because of your imperfections,
And always rise up bravely from a fall.
I am glad that you make a daily new beginning;
There is no better means of progress in the spiritual
Life than to be continually beginning afresh,
And never to think that we have done enough.

He that can have patience can have what he will. 73

The principal part of faith is patience. 139

Patience is bitter, but its fruit is sweet. 179

Lord! Who Thy thousand years dost wait 157
To work the thousandth part
Of Thy vast plan, for us create
With zeal a patient heart.

ST. TERESA'S BOOKMARK 181-T-1
Let nothing disturb thee,
Nothing affrights thee;
All things are passing;
God never changeth;
Patient endurance
Attaineth to all things;
Who God possesseth
In nothing is wanting;
Alone God sufficeth.

The greatest prayer is patience. 28

PEACE

****

Cicero wrote about 2,000 years ago that peace is liberty in tranquility. It will come to any who love God and obey His commandments.

****

A PRAYER FOR PEACE 188

Father in Heaven! Humbly before thee
Kneeling in prayer thy children appear;
We in our weakness, we in our blindness,
Thou in thy wisdom, hear us, oh hear!

God watching o'er us sleeps not nor slumbers,
Faithful night watches his angels keep,
Through all the darkness, unto the dawning,
To his beloved he giveth sleep.

Nothing can bring you peace but yourself. 63

Thy presence fills my mind with peace, 61
Brightens the thoughts so dark erewhile,
Bids care and sad foreboding cease,
Makes all things smile.

There are two ways of getting it if you want it. The first is wholly in 180
your own power; to make ourselves nests of pleasant thoughts. There are nests on the sea indeed, but safe beyond all others; only they need much art in the building. None of us yet know, for none of us have yet been taught in early youth, what fair palaces we may build of beautiful thought-proof against all adversity. Bright fancies, satisfied memories, noble histories, faithful sayings, treasure-houses of precious and restful thoughts, which care cannot disturb, nor pain make gloomy, nor poverty take away from us—houses built without hands, for our souls to live in.

If there be righteousness in the heart, 170-A
There will be beauty in the character,
If there be beauty in the character,
There will be harmony in the home.

If there be harmony in the home,
There will be order in the nation.
If there be order in the nation,
There will be peace in the world.

O God, who art Peace everlasting 181-G-1
Whose chosen reward is the gift of peace,
And who hast taught us that the peacemakers are Thy children,
Pour Thy sweet peace into our souls,
That everything discordant may utterly vanish,
And all that makes for peace be sweet to us forever.

PEACE 205

My Soul, there is a Country
Afar beyond the stars,
Where stands a winged centre
All skillful in the wars.
There, above noise and danger,
Sweet Peace sits crowned with smiles,
And One born in a manger
Commands the beauteous files.
He is thy Gracious Friend,
And (O my soul awake!)
Did in pure love descend,
To die here for thy sake.
If thou canst get but thither,
There grows the flower of peace,
The Rose that cannot wither,
Thy fortress and thy ease.
Leave then thy foolish ranges;
For none can thee secure
But One who never changes
Thy God, thy life, thy cure!

O THOU WHOSE POW'R 18

O thou whose pow'r o'er moving worlds presides,
Whose voice created, and whose wisdom guides,
On darkling man in pure effulgence shine,
And clear the clouded mind with light divine.
'Tis thine alone to calm the pious breast
With silent confidence and holy rest:
From thee, great God, we spring, to thee we tend,
Path, motive, guide, original, and end.

Grant us, O Lord, the blessing of those whose minds are stayed upon thee, that so we may be kept in perfect peace: a peace which cannot be broken. Let not our minds rest upon any creature, but only in the Creator: not upon goods, things, houses, lands, inventions of vanities or foolish fashions, lest, our peace being broken, we become cross and brittle and given over to envy. From all such deliver us, O God, and grant us thy peace. 71

Fill with inviolable peace; 209
Establish and keep my settled heart;
In Thee may all wanderings cease,
From Thee no more may I depart:
Thy utmost goodness called to prove,
Loved with an everlasting love!

PRAISE

****

Praise is simply gratitude either stated or written. But gratitude is not to be kept a secret. Share it with everyone and it will multiply.

****

HYMN 120

Lord, with glowing heart I'd praise thee
For the bliss thy love bestows,
For the pardoning grace that saves me,
And the peace that from it flows.
Help, O God! My weak endeavor,
This dull soul to rapture raise;
Thou must light the flame, or never
Can my love be warmed to praise.

Lord! This bosom's ardent feeling
Vainly should my lips express;
Low before thy foot-stool kneeling,
Design thy suppliant's prayer to bless.
Let thy grace, my soul's chief treasure,
Love's pure flame within me raise;
And, since words can never measure,
Let my life show forth thy praise.

Great art Thou, O Lord, and greatly to be praised; 181-A-6
Great is Thy power, and of Thy wisdom there is no end.
And, man, being a part of Thy creation, desires to praise Thee,
Man who bears about with him his mortality,
The witness of his sin, even the witness that Thou "resistest the proud"
Yet man, this part of Thy creation, desires to praise Thee.
Thou movest us to delight in praising Thee;
For Thou has formed us for Thyself,
And our hearts are restless till they find rest in Thee.

FOR GOD'S GLORY 181-A-6

O God, our true Life, in Whom and by Whom all things live,
Thou commandest us to seek Thee, and art ready to be found;
Thou biddest us knock, and openest when we do so.
To know Thee is life, to serve Thee is freedom,
to enjoy Thee is a kingdom,
to praise, and bless, and adore Thee, I worship Thee,
I glorify Thee, I give thanks to Thee for Thy great glory.
I humbly beseech Thee to abide with me, to reign in me,
to make this heart of mine a holy temple,
a fit habitation for Thy Divine Majesty.
O Thou Maker and Preserver of all things, visible and invisible!
keep, I beseech Thee, the work of Thine own hand,
who trusts in Thy mercy alone for safety and protection.
Guard me with the power of Thy grace, here and in all places,
now and at all times, forevermore.

When I doubt myself, remind me of my successes, 8
When I falter, strengthen me with the knowledge that I have come this far with Your help,
When I am sorrowful, bring me only a day of sunshine, a child's laughter, a single flower bud, or the sound of a simple song.
Teach me not only to be grateful, but to share my blessings with others who may not have so many as I.

THY KINGDOM COME 181-B-4

Thou hope of all the lawly!
To thirsting souls how kind!
Gracious to all who seek Thee,
Oh, what to those who find!

My tongue but lisps Thy praises,
Yet praise me my employ;
Love makes me bold to praise Thee,
For Thou art all my joy.

In Thee my soul delighting,
Findeth her only rest;
And so in Thee confiding,
May all the world be blest!

Dwell with us, and our darkness
Will flee before Thy light;
Scatter the world's deep midnight,
And fill it with delight.

O all mankind! Behold Him
And seek His love to know;
And let your hearts, in seeking,
Be fired with love and glow!

O come, O come, great Monarch,
Eternal glory Thine;
The longing world waits for Thee!
Arise, arise and shine!

Send forth, O God, thy light and truth,
And let them lead me still,
Undaunted, in the paths of right,
Up to thy holy hill;
Then to thy altar will I spring,
And in my God rejoice;
And praise shall tune the trembling string,
And gratitude my voice.

PRAISE

HOLY, HOLY, HOLY! 93
Holy, holy, holy! Though the darkness hide thee,
Though the eye of sinful man thy glory may not see,
Only thou art holy, there is none beside thee,
Perfect in power, in love, and purity.

O God the Father, who saidst at the beginning: let there be light
205
and it was so! Enlighten my eyes that I never sleep in death, lest at any time my enemy should say, I have prevailed against him.

O God the Son, Light of Light, the most true and perfect Light, from whom this light of the sun and the day had their beginning: Thou that art the light shining in darkness enlightening everyone that cometh into the world! Expel from me all clouds of ignorance, and give me true understanding, that in Thee and by Thee I may know the Father: whom to know is to love, and to serve is to reign.

O God the Holy Ghost, the Fire that enlightens and warms our hearts! Shed into me Thy most sacred light ... Ray Thyself into my soul, that I may see what an exceeding weight of Glory my enemy would bereave me of, for the mere shadows, and painting of this world.

I praise Thee while my days go on; 25
I love Thee while my days go on;
Through dark and dearth, through fire and frost.
With emptied arms and treasure lost,
I thank Thee while my days go on.

Tune me, O Lord, into one harmony 178
With Thee, one full responsive vibrant chord;
Unto Thy praise, all love and melody,
Tune me, O Lord.

Take my life, and let it be 89
Consecrated, Lord, to Thee.
Take my moments and my days;
Let them flow in ceaseless praise.

****
One's best protection is the mantle of faith, the sword of courage, and the girdle of God's omnipotent power.
****

O GOD, OUR HELP IN AGES PAST 208

O God, our help in ages past,
Our hope in years to come,
Our shelter from the stormy blast,
and our eternal home—

Under the shadow of thy throne
Thy saints have dwelt secure;
Sufficient is Thine arm alone,
And our defense is sure.

Before the hills in order stood,
Or earth received her frame,
From everlasting thou art God,
To endless years the same.

A thousand ages in thy sight
Are like an evening gone;
Short as the watch that ends the night
Before the rising sun.

Time, like an ever-rolling stream
Bears all its sons away;
They fly, forgotten, as a dream
Dies at the opening day.

Our God, our help in ages past,
Our hope in years to come,
Be thou our guard while troubles last,
And our eternal home.

O Holy Spirit, O eternal God, O Christ, O Love, come Thou into my heart; by Thy power draw it unto Thee, my God, and give me charity without fear. Protect me Thou, O ineffable Love, from every evil thought; inflame me and permeate me with Thy exquisite love, so that every pain may become a ray of light! My Holy Father and my sweet Lord, help me now in all of my ministries. Christ, Love. 181-C-1

Blessed Jesus, open your heart for those who are weak. Strengthen me with thy faith and protect me with thy mighty strength. Save me from all harm, I pray. 175

Behind the dim unknown, 135
Standeth God within the shadow,
keeping watch above his own.

PROTECTION

FOR PROTECTION 181-P-1

I bind to myself today
God's power to guide me,
God's might to uphold me,
God's wisdom to teach me,
God's ear to hear me,
God's eye to watch over me,
God's word to give me speech,
God's hand to guard me,
God's way to lie before me,
God's shield to protect me
against the snares of demons,
against the seductions of vices,
against the lusts of nature,
against those who wish me ill.
Christ, protect me today.

FOR SAFETY IN TRAVEL 181-C-2

Grant me this day a steady hand and watchful eye so that no harm will come to others as I pass by. Protect me as I go my way, and lead me safely to my destiny.

When you have closed your doors, and darkened your room, remember never to say that you are alone, for you are not alone; God is within, and your genius is within, - and what need have they of light to see what you are doing? 64

REGRETS and REPENTANCE

****

Regrets really have no worth except as a reminder of the penalty incurred when one has not been true to the conscience in one's own heart, so do not spend much time on regrets. Repentance can be a cleansing, a purifying of the spirit, giving one the energy to atone and go forward, free of guilt and regrets.

****

LAST PRAYE R 111

Father, I scarcely darn to pray,
So clear I see, now it is done,
That I have wasted half my day,
And left my work but just begun.

So clear I see that things I thought
Were right or harmless were a sin;
So clear Jsee that I have sought,
Unconscious, selfish aims to win;

So clear I see that I have hurt
The soul I might have helped to save;
That I have slothful been, inert,
Deaf to the calls thy leaders gave.

In outskirts of thy kingdom vast,
Father, the humblest spot give me;
Set me the lowliest task thou hast;
Let my repentance work for thee!

Finish every day and be done with it. You have done what you could. 63
Some blunders and absurdities no doubt crept in; forget them as soon as you can. Tomorrow is a new day; begin it well and serenely and with too high a spirit to be cumbered with your old nonsense. This day is all that is good and fair. It is too dear, with its hopes and invitations, to waste a moment on the yesterdays.

Lord, I my vows to Thee renew; 119
Disperse my sins as morning dew;
Guide my first springs of thought and will,
And with Thyself my spirit fill.

Because I spent the strength Thou gavest me 214
In struggle which Thou never didst ordain,
And have but dregs of life to offer Thee—
O Lord, I do repent.

Every man has a paradise around him till he sins, and the angel of an 133
accusing conscience drives him from his Eden.

The vain regret that sails above the wreck of squandered hours. 211

REGRETS and REPENTANCE

Dear Lord and Father of mankind, 211
Forgive our foolish ways!
Reclothe us in our rightful mind,
In purer lives Thy service find,
In deeper reverence, praise.

Drop Thy still dews of quietness,
Till all our strivings cease;
Take from our souls the strain and stress,
And let our ordered lives confess
The beauty of Thy peace.

The Moving Finger writes; and, having writ, 160
Moves on: nor all your Piety nor Wit
Shall lure it back to cancel half a Line,
Nor all your Tears wash out a Word of it.

FOR INTERCESSION 131
Hail, Queen of Heav'n, the ocean star,
Guide of the wanderer here below;
Thrown on life's surge, we calm thy care
Save us from peril and from woe.
Mother of Christ, Star of the Sea.
Pray for the wanderer, pray for me.

O gentle, chaste, and spotless Maid,
We sinners make our prayers through thee;
Remind thy Son that He has paid
The price of our iniquity.
Virgin most pure, Star of the Sea,
Pray for the sinner, pray for me.

Be it according to Thy word; 209
Redeem me from all sin;
My heart would now receive Thee, Lord,
Come in, my Lord, come in!

Regret not that which is past; and trust not to thine own righteousness. 181-A-4

There are two angels, that attend unseen 133
Each one of us, and in great books record
Our good and evil deeds. He who writes down
The good ones, after each action closes
His volume, and ascends with it to God.
The other keeps his dreadful day-book open
Til sunset, that we may repent; which doing,
The record of the action fades away,
And leaves a line of white across the page.

REGRETS and REPENTANCE

We are our own devils; we drive ourselves out of our Edens. 81

THREE THINGS COME NOT BACK 74-A

Remember, three things come not back:
The arrow sent upon its track -
It will not swerve, it will not stay
Its speed; it flies to wound, or slay.
The spoken word so soon forgot
By thee - but it has perished not;
In other hearts 'tis living still,
And doing work for good or ill.
And the lost opportunity
That cometh back no more to thee.
In vain thou weepest, in vain dost yearn--
Those three will never more return.

I sent my soul through the invisible 160
Some letter of that after-life to spell:
And by and by my soul returned to me,
And answered, "I myself am heaven and hell."

I never did repent for doing good, nor shall not now. 186

Repentance is a hearty sorrow for our past misdeeds, and a sincere resolution and endeavor, to the utmost of our power, to conform all our actions to the law of God. I t does not consist in one single act of sorrow, but in doing works meet for repentance; in a sincere obedience to the law of Christ for the remainder of our lives. 132

God hath promised pardon to him that repenteth, but he hath not promised repentance to him that sinneth. 181-A-3

There is one case of death-bed repentance recorded, that of the pentitent thief, that none should despair; and only one that none should presume. 181·A·6

You cannot repent too soon, because you do not know how soon it may be too late. 76

Our repentance is not so much regret for the ill we have done as fear of ill that may happen to us in consequence. 126

SERENITY

****

That calm, quiet, placid peace of mind and spirit surrounds those who live by what they know to be the truest guide to a comfortable and contented life—treat all people as you wish to be treated.

****

It is in your power to withdraw into yourself whenever you desire. 12
Perfect tranquility within consists in the good ordering of the mind—the realm of your own.

Our days are numbered: let us spare 84
Our anxious hearts a needless care:
Tis Thine to number out our days;
Tis ours to give them to Thy praise.

Every lot is happy to a person who bears it with tranquility. 18

Great tranquility of heart is his who cares for neither praise nor blame. 118

My conscience is my crown, 192
Contented thoughts my rest;
My heart is happy in itself;
My bliss is in my breast.

Serene will be our days and bright. 215
And happy will our nature be,
When love is an unerring light,
And joy its own security.

TO MAKE THIS LIFE WORTH WHILE 60
May every soul that touches mine-
Be it the slightest contact -
Get there from some good;
Some little grace; one kindly thought;
One aspiration yet unfelt;
One bit of courage
For the darkening sky;
One gleam of faith
To brave the thickening ills of life;
One glimpse of brighter skies
Beyond the gathering mists -
To make this life worth while.

Lord, be Thou near and cheer my lonely way; 46
With thy sweet peace my aching bosom fill;
Scatter my cares and fears; my grieves allay,
And be it mine each day
To love and please Thee still.

SERENITY

Holy Spirit, Peace divine! 134
Still this restless heart of mine;
Speak to calm this tossing sea,
Stayed in Thy tranquility.

> The little cares that fretted me, 8
> I lost them yesterday.
> Among the fields above the sea,
> Among the winds at play.
> Among the lowing of the herds,
> The rustling of the trees,
> Among the singing of the birds
> The humming of the bees.
> The foolish fears of what might pass
> I cast them all away
> Among the clover-scented grass,
> Among the new-mown hay,
> Among the hushing of the corn
> Where drowsy poppies nod,
> Where ill thoughts die and good are born...
> Out in the fields with God.

We praise thee, O God, for thy power and thy peace; for the strong pressure of thy will; for the deep and tranquil spirit which is thy presence. Each morning we entrust ourselves to thy faithfulness, each night to thine invincible rest: O thou who are mightier than our needs. 8

Peace does not dwell in outward things, but within the soul; we may preserve it in the midst of the bitterest pain, if our will remain firm and submissive. Peace in this life springs from acquiescence, not in an exemption from suffering. 69

SPIRITUAL GROWTH

****

The spirit grows with tender loving care. Provide it with the fruit of loving others, the meat of God's blessings, and the dessert of a clear conscious.

****

FOR CHRIST-LIKENESS 181-B-5

O Lord Jesus, acknowledge what is Thine in us, and take away from us all that is not Thine; for Thy honor and glory.

FOR GOD'S LOVE 181-B-4

O God,
Your greatness knows no bounds,
Your peace goes beyond all understanding,
Your love surpasses all reckoning.
Help us to love you
If not as you have first loved us,
Then to the fullness of our power to love.
And strengthen and deepen this power
So that we may love you more and more.

FOR A HOLY LIFE 181-B-2

Open our hearts, O Lord,
and enlighten us by the grace of your Holy Spirit,
that we may always seek what is pleasing to you
and order our lives after your commandments
that we may be worthy to enter into your unending joy.

FOR PURIFICATION 181-B-1

Lord our God, great, eternal, wonderful in glory,
who keepest covenant and promises for those
that love Thee with their whole heart,
who art the life of all,
the help of those that flee unto Thee,
cleanse us from our sins, secret and open;
and from every thought displeasing to Thy goodness,
cleanse our bodies and souls,
our hearts and consciences,
that with a pure heart, and a clear soul,
with perfect love and calm hope,
we may venture confidently and fearlessly to pray unto thee.

Lord, for the erring thought 103
Not into evil wrought;
Lord, for the wicked will
Betrayed and baffled still;
For the heart from itself kept,
Our Thanksgiving accept.

FOR SPIRITUAL BLESSINGS 175

Holy God, I come to ask thy blessing for my empty heart and tired soul. I am enmeshed in the world, its ways, its habits, its vanities. Help me to become less interested in material things, and more concerned in the search for the peace of mind and joy which comes with true faith in the goodness of God. Grant me the grace to be zealous in this resolution to turn my will and my life over to His care. I pray for the strength and ability to pursue the path of godliness, with the assurance that my new heart and my revived spirit will be filled with the magnificent gifts which come to all who love God fully.

TO INCREASE ONE'S FAITH 181-C-3

Glory and Praise be to Thee, Most loving Jesus Christ.
From all evils, past, present and to come, deliver me.
Do Thou, by Thy most bitter death,
Give me a lively faith, firm hope, a perfect charity.
That with my whole soul I may love Thee,
With all my soul, and with all my strength.
Firm and steadfast in good works make me,
and in Thy service make to persevere,
so that I may be able always to please Thee, Lord Jesus Christ.

Lord it is my chief complaint, 48
That my love is weak and faint;
Yet I love Thee and adore, -
Oh, for grace to love Thee more!

O Lord! thou art greater than our thoughts of thee. 16
Thou are to us more than we can speak.
Thou dost also transcend our utmost conception.
All of thy name that we can frame into words is but little;
and all of thee that we can frame into emotions is still but little;
and all that we can conceive of thee by the imagination is yet but
very little.
Beyond our thoughts and feelings and conceptions thou dost stretch
endlessly and boundlessly.
We look toward thee as men look toward the morning.
Thou art our sun: thou art our Light; thou art our Life.
In thee our life is hid.

STRENGTH and POWER

****

Strength is natural for those who are strong in their faith in God's goodness. It is weakened by fear, guilt, and sin.

****

A PRAYER 22

My God (oh, let me call thee mine,
Weak, wretched sinner though I be).
My trembling soul would fain be Thine;
My feeble faith still clings to Thee.

Not only for the past I grieve,
The future fills me with dismay;
Unless Thou hasten to relieve,
Thy suppliant is a castaway.

I cannot say my faith is strong.
I dare not hope my love is great;
But strength and love to Thee belong:
Oh, do not leave me desolate!

I know I owe my all to Thee;
Oh, take the heart I cannot give;
Do Thou my Strength, my Saviour be,
And make me to Thy glory live!

Almighty and merciful God who art the Strength of the weak, the 85
Refreshment of the weary, the Comfort of the sad, the Help of the tempted, the Life of the Dying, the God of patience and of all consolation; Thou knowest full well the inner weakness of our nature, how we tremble and quiver before pain, and cannot bear the cross without Thy Divine help and support. Help me, then, an eternal and pitying God, help me to possess my soul in patience, to maintain unshaken hope in Thee, to keep the childlike trust which feels a Father's heart hidden beneath the cross; so shall I be strengthened with power according to Thy glorious might, in all patience and long suffering; I shall be enabled to endure pain and temptation, and, in the very depth of my suffering, to praise Thee with a joyful heart.

O Lord God Almighty, who gives power to the faint, and increasest 113
strength to them that have no might, without Thee I can do nothing, but by Thy gracious assistance I am enabled for the performance of every duty laid upon me. Lord of power and love, I come, trusting in Thine almighty strength, and Thine infinite goodness, to beg from Thee what is wanting in myself; even that grace which shall help me such to be, and such to do, as Thou wouldest have me. O my God, let Thy grace be sufficient for me, and ever present with me, that I may do all things as I ought. I will trust in Thee, in who is my everlasting strength. Be Thou my Helper, to carry me on beyond my own strength, and to make all that I think, and speak, and do: acceptable in Thy sight, through Jesus Christ.

STRENGTH and POWER

STRENGTHEN ME IN THIS HOUR 66
Blessed art Thou, O Lord our God, who dwellest in the highest, Thou whom the angels and all the powers of heaven praise and exalt unceasingly. Thy weak and lowly handmaiden calls upon Thee, who regardest the humble; strengthen me this hour with the power of Thy Holy Spirit, and show the wicked enemy of Christ that Thou art the God who didst send Thine angel to the three youths and didst drive the flame of fire out of the furnace. Hear my prayer, O Lord, send me Thine aid. Be not mindful of my sins and unworthiness; but, remembering Thy mercy and Thy readiness in helping them that call upon Thee, save me in this hour of my distress for the sake of Jesus Christ, Thy only Son, Our Lord.

Self-reverence, self-knowledge, self-control, 200
These three alone lead life to sovereign power.

Leaning on Him, make with reverent meekness 211
His own thy will,
And with strength from Him shall thy utter weakness
Life's task fulfill.

Hear my prayer according to thy faithfulness; answer me according to 181-P-2
thy justice. My spirit grows faint and my heart grows numb. I stretch out my arms to thee, asking thy speedy mercy. Show me the way I should go, deliver me from my foes, and teach me to do thy will. Let faithfulness spring from my heart and contentment overpower my spirit so that I may go forth restored by love, confident that all my undertakings which are begun in sincerity will come to a quick and satisfactory conclusion.

Give me whatever you ask of me. 181-A-6
Then ask of me what you will, Lord.
Remember that we are only dust,
For of the dust you made us.
But I can do anything in Him who strengthens me;
Lord, strengthen me, and I can do everything.
Give me whatever you ask of me,
Then ask of me what you will.

Accept, O God, my plea. Awaken my conscious will and energy, for I 175
know there is hidden strength within me to overcome all obstacles and temptations. Do not let my small defeats and discouragements delay me in my determination to succeed in whatever I do. I know that I can overcome failure and disappointment, and with thy help, become a stronger, sturdier, and more disciplined person.

Nothing is as strong as gentleness. Nothing is as gentle as real strength. 181-F-1

TIME

****
Today is all the time we have—yesterday cannot be recalled or relived, there is no assurance of a tomorrow, so only today is truly ours to use as we wish. Make it a good one.
****

FOR THE USE OF TIME 115

O Lord, in whose hands are life and death,
By Whose power I am sustained, and by whose mercy I am spared,
Look down upon me with pity.
Forgive me that I have until now so much neglected the duty which
Thou hast assigned to me, and suffered the days and hours of which
I must give account to pass away without any endeavor to accomplish
Thy will.
Make me to remember, O God that every day is Thy gift,
And ought to be used according to Thy command.
Grant me, therefore, so to repent of my negligence,
That I may obtain mercy from Thee,
And pass the time which Thou shalt yet allow me in diligent
Performance of Thy commands; through Jesus Christ.

THE TIME 39

There is a time for some things,
And a time for all things;
A time for great things
And a time for small things.

Dost thou love life? Then do not squander time; for that's the stuff life is made of. 73

If time be of all things the most precious, wasting time must be the greatest prodigality; since lost time is never found again and what we call time enough always proved little enough. Let us then be up and doing, and doing to the purpose; so by diligence shall we do more with less perplexity. Sloth makes all things difficult, but industry all easy.

Employ thy time well, if thou meanest to gain leisure. Since thou are not sure of a minute, throw not away an hour.

Life is too short to waste 63
'Twill soon be dark;
Up! Mind thine own aim, and
God speed the mark!

Time cures sorrows and squabbles because we all change, and are no longer the same persons. Neither the offender nor the offended is the same. 165

When time, who steals our years away, 181-T-4
Shall steal our pleasures, too,
The mem'ry of the past will stay,
And half our joys renew.

TIME

I have only just a minute, 8
Only sixty seconds in it.
Forced upon me - can't refuse it.
But it's up to me to use it.
I must suffer if I lose it.
Give account if I abuse it.
Just a tiny little minute,
But eternity is in it.

Procrastination is the thief of time. 217

Take time to work - it is the price of success; 8
Take time to think - it is the source of power;
Take time to play - it is the sécret of perpetual youth;
Take time to read - it is the foundation of wisdom;
Take time to worship - it is the highway to reverence;
Take time to be friendly - it is the road to happiness;
Take time to dream - it is hitching our wagon to a star;
Take time to love and be loved - it is the privilege of the gods.

To every thing there is a season, and a time to every purpose under the heaven: 20-A
A time to be born, and a time to die; a time to plant, and a time to pluck up that which is planted;
A time to kill, and a time to heal; a time to break down, and a time to build up;
A time to weep, and a time to laugh; a time to mourn, and a time to dance;
A time to cast away stones and a time to gather stones together;
A time to embrace, and a time to refrain from embracing;
A time to get, and a time to lose; a time to keep, and a time to cast away;
A time to rend, and a time to sew; a time to keep-silence, and a time to speak;
A time to love, and a time to hate; a time of war, and a time of peace.

WHAT TIME IS IT? 8

What time is it?
Time to do well,
Time to live better,
Give up that grudge,
Answer that letter,
Speak the kind word to sweeten a sorrow,
Do that kind deed you would leave 'till tomorrow.

TRADITIONAL PRAYERS and DEVOTIONS

****

Here are a few of the prayers known to all. They will provide every need—comfort, solace, inspiration, and guidance on the path of righteousness.

****

THE LORD'S PRAYER (OUR FATHER) 20-A

Our Father, who art in heaven,
hallowed be thy name;
thy kingdom come;
thy will be done on earth as it is in heaven.
Give us this day our daily bread,
And forgive us our trespasses,
as we forgive those who trespass against us;
and lead us not into temptations;
but deliver us from evil.

THE LORD'S PRAYER OF ISLAM 20-C

In the name of Allah, the Beneficent, the Merciful!
Praise be to Allah, Lord of the Worlds,
The Beneficent, the Merciful,
Ruler of the Day of Judgment,
Thee alone we worship; Thee alone we ask for help.
Show us the straight path,
The path of those whom Thou hast favored;
Not of those who have earned Thine anger
Nor of those who go astray.

THE TEN COMMANDMENTS 20-A

I am the Lord thy God... Thou shalt have no other gods before Me... Thou shalt not make unto thee a graven image... Thou shalt not take the name of the Lord thy God in vain... Remember the sabbath day, to keep it holy... Honor thy father and thy mother... Thou shalt nor murder... Thou shalt not commit adultery... Thou shalt not steal...
Thou shalt not hear false witness... Thou shalt not covet...

THE UNITY 20-C

In the name of Allah, the Beneficent, the Merciful!
Say: He is Allah, the One!
Allah, the eternally besought of all!
He begetteth not nor was begotten.
And there is none comparable unto him.

GLORY BE 20-B

Glory be to the Father, and to the Son,
and to the Holy Ghost.
As it was in the beginning, is now,
and ever shall be, world without end.

ACT OF HOPE 20-B
O my God, relying on Thy gracious promises, I hope, by the merits of Jesus Christ, for the pardon of my sins, grace to serve Thee faithfully in this life by doing the good works which Thou have commanded, and eternal happiness in the world to come, through Jesus Christ, our Lord.

ACT OF CHARITY 20-B
O my Lord, I love Thee with my whole heart, and above all things, because Thou art infinitely good in thyself and infinitely to be loved; and for Thy Sake I love my neighbor as myself.

ANGELICAL SALUTATION 20-B

Hail Mary, full of Grace,
Blessed art Thou amongst women,
And blessed is the fruit of Thy womb Jesus.
Holy Mary, Mother of God,
Pray for us sinners,
Now and at the hour of our death.

THE APOSTLES' CREED 20-B
I believe in God, the Father Almighty, Creator of heaven and earth; in Jesus Christ, His only Son, our Lord, who was conceived by the Holy Ghost, born of the Virgin Mary, suffered under Pontius Pilate, was crucified, died, and was buried. He descended into hell, the third day He rose again from the dead, He ascended into heaven, sitteth at the right hand of God, the Father Almighty; from thence He shall come to judge the living and the dead, I believe in the Holy Ghost, the Holy catholic church; the communion of Saints; the forgiveness of sin, the resurrection of the body; and life everlasting. Amen.

BEFORE A CRUCIFIX 20-B
O good and dearest Jesus, before thy face I humbly kneel, and with the most fervent desire of soul, I pray and beseech thee to impress upon my heart lively sentiments of faith, hope, and charity, true sorrow for my sins, and a true desire of amendment, while with deep affection and grief of soul I reflect upon and ponder over Thy five most precious wounds, having before my eyes the words of David, the prophet, "They have pierced my hands and feet, they have numbered all my bones."

FOR ALL SAINTS 20-B
We give thanks to thee, O Lord, for all saints and servants of Thine, who have done justly, loved mercy, and walked humbly with their God. For all the high and holy ones, who have wrought wonders and gained great fame, we thank thee. For all the meek and lowly ones, who have earnestly sought thee in darkness, and held fast their faith in trial, and done well to all men as they had opportunity, we thank thee. As they have comforted and upheld our souls, grant us grace to follow in their steps, and at last to share with them in the inheritance of the saints in light.

TRADITIONAL PRAYERS and DEVOTIONS

THE BEATITUDES 20-A

Blessed are the poor in spirit, for theirs is the kingdom of heaven.
Blessed are they that mourn; for they shall be comforted.
Blessed are the meek; for they shall inherit the earth.
Blessed are they which do hunger and thirst after righteousness; for they shall be filled.
Blessed are the merciful; for they shall obtain mercy.
Blessed are the pure in heart; for they shall see God.
Blessed are the peacemakers; for they shall be called the children of God.
Blessed are they which are persecuted for righteousness' sake, for theirs is the kingdom of heaven.

ST. FRANCIS' PRAYER 181-F-2

Lord, make me an instrument of your peace.
Where there is hatred, let me sow love.
Where there is injury, pardon.
Where there is doubt, faith.
Where there is despair, hope.
Where there is darkness, light.
And where there is sadness, joy.
O Divine Master, grant that I may not so much seek to be consoled, as to console,
To be understood, as to understand,
To be loved, as to love,
For it is in giving that we receive,
It is in pardoning that we are pardoned,
And it is in dying that we are born to eternal life.

TWENTY THIRD PSALM 20-A

The Lord is my shepherd; I shall not want.
He maketh me to lie down in green pastures; he leadeth me beside the still waters.
He restoreth my soul: he leadeth me in the paths of righteousness for his name's sake.
Yea, though I walk through the valley of the shadow of death, I will fear no evil; for thou art with me; thy rod and thy staff they comfort me.
Thou preparest a table before me in the presence of mine enemies: thou anointest my head with oil: my cup runneth over.
Surely goodness and mercy shall follow me all the days of my life: and I will dwell in the house of the Lord for ever.

VIRTUES and VICES

****
There is so much good in the worst of us,
And so much bad in the best of us,
That it ill behooves any of us
To find fault with the rest of us. *Unknown*
****

Be trustful, be steadfast, whatever betide thee. 8
Only one thing do thou ask of the Lord,
Grace to go forward wherever He guides thee,
Simply believing the truth of His word.

My life is but the weaving 8
Between my God and me.
I only choose the colors
He weaveth steadily.
Sometimes He weaveth sorrow
And I in foolish pride,
Forget He sees the upper
And I the under side.

Whatsoever things are true, 20-A
whatsoever things are honest,
whatsoever things are just,
whatsoever things are pure,
whatsoever things are lovely,
whatsoever things are of good report;
If there be any virtue,
and if there be any praise, think on these things

Give strength, give thought, give deed, give wealth; 8
Give love, give tears and give thyself.
Give, give, be always giving.
Who gives not is not living;
The more you give, the more you live.

Give us grace and strength to forbear and to persevere. 195
Give us courage and gaiety and the quiet man,
Spare to us our friends, soften to us our enemies.

Faithfully faithful to every trust. 8
Honestly honest in every deed.
Righteously righteous and justly just:
This is the whole of the good man's creed.

No sinful word, nor deed of wrong 181-A-2
Nor thoughts that idly rove;
But simple truth be on our tongue,
And in our hearts be love.

VIRTUES and VICES

Purge from our hearts the stains so deep and foul, 8
Of wrath and pride and care;
Send Thine own holy calm upon the soul,
And bid it settle there!

Loving looks the large-eyed cow 139
Loving stares the long-eared ass
At Heaven's glory in the grass!
Child, with added human birth,
Come to bring the child of earth
Glad repentance, cheerful mirth,
And a seat beside the hearth
At the Father's knee.

Make us peaceful as the cow;
Make us patient as the ass;
Make us quiet as thou art now;
Make us strong as thou wilt be.
Make us always know and see
We are His as well as thou.

May I be no man's enemy, and may I be the friend of that which is 67
eternal and abides. May I never quarrel with those nearest me; and if I do, may I be reconciled quickly. May I never devise evil against any man; if any man devise evil against me, may I escape uninjured and without the need of hurting him. May I love, seek, and attain only that which is good. May I wish for all men's happiness and envy none. May I never rejoice in the ill-fortune of one who has wronged me. When I have done or said what is wrong, may I never wait for the rebuke of others, but always rebuke myself until I make amends.
May I win no victory that harms either me or my opponent.
May I reconcile friends who are wroth with one another. May I, to the extent of my power, give all needful help to my friends and to all who are in want. May I never fail a friend in danger. When visiting those in grief may I be able by gentle and healing words to soften their pain.
May I respect myself.
May I always keep tame that which rages within me.
May I accustom myself to be gentle, and never be angry with people because of circumstances. May I never discuss who is wicked and what wicked things he has done, but know good men and follow in their footsteps.

Give me beauty in the inward soul; and may the inward and the outer 190
be at one. May I reckon wisdom to be wealth, and may I have so much gold as a temperate man and only he can bear and carry.
This prayer, I think is enough for me.

Oh, great Father, never let me judge another man until I have walked 109
in his moccasins for two weeks.

HATE 8

Anything, God, but hate.
I have known it in my day,
And the best it does is scar your soul
And eat your heart away.
Man must know more than hate,
As the years go rolling on;
For the stars survive and the spring survives,
Only man denies the dawn.
God, if I have but one prayer
Before the cloud-wrapped end,
I'm sick of hate and the waste it makes.
Let me be my brother's friend.

This above all; to Thine own self be true, 186
And it must follow, as the night the day,
Thou canst not then be false to any man.

He that does well to another does well also to himself, not only in the consequences, but in the very act; for the consciousness of well doing is, in itself, ample reward. 185

What stronger breastplate than a heart untainted! 186
Thrice is he armed that hath his quarrel just;
And he but naked, though locked up in steel,
Whose conscience with injustice is corrupted.

Live among men as if God were watching. 185
Talk to God as if men were listening.

Love, hope, fear, faith - these make humanity; 26
These are its sign, and note of character.

You will find it less easy to uproot faults, than to choke them by gaining virtues. Do not think of your faults; still less of other's faults; in every person who comes near you look for what is good and strong; honor that; rejoice in it; and, as you can, try to imitate it; and your faults will drop off, like dead leaves, when their time comes. 180

This is the punishment of the liar; he is not believed, even when he speaks the truth. 20-G

God hath yoked to guilt, her pale tormenter, misery. 27

When befriended, remember it; 73
When you befriend, forget it.

Sin is not hurtful because it is forbidden, but it is forbidden because it is hurtful. Nor is a duty beneficial because it is commanded, but it is commanded because it is beneficial. 73

VIRTUES and VICES

Help us, O Lord, with patient love to bear 8
Each others faults, to suffer with true meekness;
Help us each other's joys and grieves to share,
But let us turn to Thee alone in weakness.

O God, who through thy Son Jesus Christ hast promised a blessing to the 122
meek upon the earth: Take from us all pride and vanity, boasting and forwardness, and give us the true courage that shows itself by gentleness, the true wisdom that shows itself by simplicity, and the true power that shows itself by modesty; for Christ's sake.

Make us of one heart and mind; 209
Courteous, pitiful, and kind;
Lowly, meek, in thought and word,
Altogether like our Lord.

FOR RELEASE FROM OBSTINACY 175

O Blessed Jesus; deliver me from futile hopes and struggles against insurmountable odds. Let me realize that faith in one's ability to conquer obstacles should remain firm, but give me the humility to acknowledge that there are objectives which are beyond my reach. Do not let me cling to impossible dreams instead of turning to productive work toward achieving small successes which will bring ever-widening horizons to my life.

THE POET'S PRAYER 211

If there be some weaker one,
Give me strength to help him on;
If a blinder soul there be,
Let me guide him nearer Thee;
Make my mortal dreams come true
With the work I fain would do;
Clothe with life the weak intent,
Let me be the thing I meant;
Let me find in Thy employ,
Peace that dearer is than joy;
Out of self to love be led,
And to heaven acclimated;
Until all things sweet and good
Seem my natural habitude.

My prayer is to conquer pride with humility, wrath with love, anxiety with 175
calmness and confidence, selfishness by generosity, ignorance by learning, evil by doing good, and restlessness with the peace which closeness to God bestows upon me.

Search thine own heart. What paineth thee 211
In others, in thyself may be;
All dust is frail, all flesh is weak;
Be thou the true man thou dost seek.

VIRTUES and VICES

FOR GENEROSITY 199
O God, Who hast called us to open our hand, and Thou wouldst fill it,
and we would not;
open Thou not only our hand, but our heart also;
that we may know nothing but Thee,
count all things lost in comparison of Thee,
and endeavor to be made like unto Thee;
through Jesus Christ our Lord.

Love those who reprove thee, and despise those who flatter thee; for reproof may lead thee to eternal life, flattery to destruction. 20-G

Not what we give, but what we share, 135
For the gift without the giver is bare:
Who gives himself with his alms feeds three,
Himself, his hungering neighbor, and Me.

More helpful than all wisdom is one draught of simple human pity that will not forsake us. 60

The dice of God are always loaded. Every secret is told, every crime is punished, every virtue rewarded, every wrong redressed, in silence and certainty. The thief steals from himself. The swindler swindles himself. 63

God has delivered yourself to your care, and says: I had no one fitter to trust than you. Preserve this person for me such as he is by nature; modest, beautiful, faithful, noble, tranquil. 64

Let us faithfully transmit to posterity the example of virtue which we have received from our forefathers. 181-P-3

Every minute you are angry you lose sixty seconds of happiness. 8

Give me simple laboring folk, 201
Who love their work,
Whose virtue is a song
To cheer God along.

If you would cure anger, do not feed it. Say to yourself: 64
"I used to be angry every day; then every other day; now
only every third or fourth day." When you reach thirty days,
offer a sacrifice of thanksgiving to the gods.

Dost thou ask when comes His hour? 8
Then, when it shall aid thee best.
Trust His faithfulness and power,
Trust in Him, and quiet rest.

VIRTUES and VICES

Not sharp revenge, nor hell itself can find a fiercer torment than a guilty mind. 57

When the truth shines out in the soul, and the soul sees itself in the truth, there is nothing brighter than the light or more impressive than that testimony. And when the splendor of this beauty fills the entire heart, it naturally becomes visible, just as a lamp under a bowl or a light in darkness are not there to be hidden. Shining out like rays upon the body, it makes it a mirror of itself so that its beauty appears in a man's every action, his speech, his looks, his movements and his smile. 181-B-4

When we cannot see our way, 8
Let us trust and still obey;
He who bids us forward goes,
Cannot fail the way to show.
Though the sea be deep and wide,
Though a passage seem denied;
Fearless let us still proceed,
Since the Lord vouchsafes to lead.

PRAYER 175

God, if my life is filled with love and laughter,
I shall have no fear of what comes after.
I ask for three days of perfect bliss.
Few of us have more than this.
Fill my life with gay songs to sing,
And I will need no other thing_
When I die, cast me into deepest hell
If I have not lived life well.
But if my life is filled with love and laughter,
I shall have no fear of what comes after.

Be sober, be vigilant; because your adversary the devil, as a roaring lion, walketh about, seeking whom he may devour. 20-A

There is nothing evil saved that which perverts the mind and shackles the conscience. 181-A-2

WEALTH and SUCCESS

****

Wealth and success really have nothing to do with each other. While an abundance of the world's goods can make life's rocky road a bit smoother, it is not a prerequisite for a fulfilling, happy life. True success comes from within—built bit by bit with blocks of kindness, truth, faith, and love.

****

O God, the Life of the Faithful, the Bliss of the Righteous, 181-G-1
mercifully receive the prayers of Thy suppliants,
that the souls which thirst for Thy promises may
evermore be filled from Thy abundance.

There is nothing that makes men rich and strong but that which they carry inside of them. True wealth is of the heart, not of the hand. 152

Thou, O Lord, provideth enough for all men with Thy most liberal and bounteous hand, but whereas Thy gifts are, in respect to Thy goodness and free favor, made common to all men, we through our haughtiness, niggardships and distrust, do make them private and peculiar. Correct Thou the thing which our iniquity hath put out of order, and let Thy goodness supply that which our niggardliness hath plucked away. 62

The men whom I have seen succeed have always been cheerful and hopeful, who went about their business with a smile on their faces, and took the changes and chances of this mortal life like men. 122

Self-trust is the first secret of success. 63

Why should we be in such desperate haste to succeed, and in such desperate enterprises? If a man does not keep pace with his companions, perhaps it is because he hears a different drummer. 201

To find his place and fill it is success for a man. 24

If you wish success in life. make perseverance your bosom friend, experience your wise counselor, caution your elder brother, and hope your guardian genius. 2

Not in the clamor of the crowded street, 133
Not In the shouts and plaudits of the throng.
But in ourselves are triumph and defeat.

Gold can buy nearly everything in this world, except that which a man wants most happiness. 8

WISDOM

****

Seneca, Roman philosopher of the first century, said, "Wisdom teaches us to do, as well as talk, and to make our words and actions all of a color."

****

Wisdom is the principle thing; therefore get wisdom: and with all thy getting get understanding. 20-A

To make no mistakes is not in the power of man; but from their errors and mistakes the wise and good learn wisdom for the future. 168

Let us learn upon earth, those things which can prepare us for heaven. 181-J-1

It's wiser being good than bad; 26
It's safer being meek than fierce;
It's fitter being sane than mad.

I sit beside my lonely fire 4
And pray for wisdom yet;
For calmness to remember
Or courage to forget.

ETHICAL WISDOM 20-F

All desires should be abandoned,
But if you cannot abandon them,
Let your desire be for salvation.
That is the cure for it...
An excellent man, like precious metal,
Is in every way invariable;
A villain, like a scale,
Is always varying, upwards and downwards.

To have a low opinion of our own merits and to think highly of others is an evidence of wisdom. 118

Even a fool, when he holdeth his peace, is counted wise. 20-A

Well, God give them wisdom that have it: 186
and those that are fools, let them use their talents.

The wise man endeavors to shine in himself; the fool to outshine others. 2
The first is humbled by the sense of his own infirmities; the last is lifted up by the discovery of those which he observes in other men. The wise man considers what he wants and the fool what he abounds in. The wise man is happy when he gains his own approbation and the fool when he recommends himself to the applause of those about him.

WORK

****

Family may become distant, friends may desert you, and that special love may always be just outside your grasp, but a day of worthwhile and satisfying work is a great blessing. Whatever chore one must do, do it to the best of one's abilities and it will enhance each and every day.

****

Thank God every morning when you get up that you have something to do that day which must be done, whether you like it or not. Being forced to work and forced to do your best will breed in you temperance and self-control, diligence and strength of will, cheerfulness and content, and a hundred virtues which the idle never know. 122

Pray to God at the beginning of thy works, that so thou mayest bring them to a good ending. 216

Labor is life; from the inmost heart of the worker rises his God-given force, the sacred celestial life-essence breathed into him by Almighty God! 36

> Take my hands, and let them move 89
> At the impulse of Thy love.
> Take my feet, and let them be
> Swift and "beautiful" for Thee
> Take my intellect, and use
> Every power as Thou shalt choose.

Work and thou canst not escape the reward; whether thy work be fine or coarse, planting corn or writing epics, so only it be honest work, done to thine own approbation, it shall earn a reward to the senses as well as to the thought. No matter how often defeated, you are born to victory. The reward of a thing well done is to have done it. 63

Be always employed about some rational thing, that the devil find thee not idle. 181-J-1

All the performances of human art, at which we look with praise and wonder, are instances of the resistless force of perseverance. 116

He that hope hereafter to look back with satisfaction upon past years, must learn to know the present value of single minutes, and endeavor to let no particle of time fall useless to the ground. 115

LEND A HAND 86

> Look up! And not down.
> Out! And not in;
> Forward! And not back;
> And lend a hand.

A useless life is only an early death. 81

WORK

Help thy brother's boat across, and lo! thine own has reached the shore. 170-C

Good words shall gain you honor in the market-place: but good deeds shall gain you friends among men. 125

Be always employed about some rational thing, that the devil finds thee not idle. 181-J-1

> O Glorious St. Joseph, model of all who labor, 8
> obtain for me the grace to work conscientiously,
> placing love of duty before frivolous inclinations;
> to gratefully work to develop the gifts received from God,
> to work methodically, peacefully, in moderation and patience.
> Let me not shrink from difficult work for it is through
> struggle that unused talents are developed.
> Let me do my tasks well, with my best efforts,
> And permit me not to be vain in my success.
> To imitate thee shall be my desire for life and eternity.

O Lord God, when Thou givest to Thy servants to endeavor any great matter, grant us also to know that it is not the beginning, but the continuing of the same, until it be thoroughly finished, which yieldeth the true glory. 56

> Long though my task may be, cometh the end. 8
> God 'tis that helpeth me,
> His is the work, and He new strength will lend.

Blessed is the one who is too busy to worry in the daytime and too sleepy to worry at night. 8

You and I toiling for earth, may at the same time be toiling for heaven, and every day's work may be a Jacob's ladder reaching up nearer God. 164

> I see Thy aid, I ask direction, 8
> Teach me to do what pleaseth Thee;
> I can bear toil, endure affliction,
> Only Thy leadings let me see.

Grant us grace, O Lord, to work while it is day, fulfilling diligently and patiently whatever duty thou appointest us; doing small things in the day of small things, and great labors if thou summonest us to any; rising and working, or sitting still and suffering, according to Thy word. 178

It never occurs to fools that merit and good fortune are closely united. 81

Good for the body is the work of the body. Good for the soul the work of the soul. And good for either the work of the other. 201

WORK

No man is born into the world whose work 135
Is not born with him. There is always work,
And tools to work withal, for those who will;
And blessed are the horny hands of toil!

If I can stop one heart from breaking, 52
I shall not live in vain.
If I can ease one life the aching,
Or cool one pain,
Or help one fainting robin
Unto his nest again.
I shall not live in vain.

Teach us, good Lord, to serve Thee as Thou deservest, 181-I-1
To give and not to count the cost;
To fight and not to heed the wounds,
To toil and not to seek for rest;
To labor and not ask for any reward
Save that of knowing that we do Thy will.

To the man who himself strives earnestly, God also lends a helping hand. 3

When God wanted sponges and oysters, He made them and put one on a rock, and the other in the mud. When He made man, He did not make him to be a sponge or an oyster; He made him with feet and hands, and head, and heart, and vital blood, and a place to use them and said to him, "Go, work!" 16

God be thank'd that the dead have left still 150
Good undone for the living to do -
Still some aim for the heart and the will
And the soul of a man to pursue.

Greater even than the pious man is he who eats that which is the fruit of his own toil; for Scripture declares him twice-blessed. 20-G

Men give me some credit for genius. All the genius I have lies just in this: When I have a subject in hand, I study it profoundly. Day and night it is before me. I explore it in all its bearings. My mind becomes pervaded with it. Then the effort which I make the people are pleased to call the fruit of genius. It is the fruit of labor and thought. 87

YOUTH, AGE and MEMORIES

****
When we're young, we wish we were older. When we become old, we spend many hours dreaming of our youth. Such time would be better spent making the very best of this day. But time used remembering the good times of the past is not lost or wasted, for sweet memories are joys renewed.
****

Long, long be my heart with such memories fill'd! 181-T-4
Like the vase in which roses have one been distill'd;
You may break; you may shatter the vase if you will,
But the scent of the roses will hang round it still.

Memory, like books which remain a long time shut up in the dust, 185
needs to be opened from time to time; it is necessary, so to speak, to open
its leaves, that it may be ready in time of need.

A land of promise, a land of memory, 200
A land of promise flowing with the milk
And honey of delicious memories!

Life's best days are not those to which we look forward with most 203
expectation of happiness, but those to which we may look back with most
of gladness. They are the days which stand the test of experience and
reminiscence.

Old age has been charged with being insensible to pleasure and to the 40
enjoyments arising from the gratification of the senses—a most blessed
and heavenly effect, truly, if it eases us of what in youth was the sorest
plague of life.

To know how to grow old is the master-work of Wisdom, and one of 6
the most difficult chapters in the great art of living.

Age is a quality of mind; 8
If you've left your dreams behind,
If hope is cold,
If you no longer look ahead,
If your ambitious fires are dead,
Then, you are old!

But if from life you take the best,
And if in life you keep the jest,
If love you hold;
No matter how the years go by,
No matter how the birthdays fly—
You are not old.

It is not just when a villainous act has been committed that it torments 179
us; it is when we think of it afterward, for the remembrance of it lasts
forever.

AUTHOR INDEX

AUTHOR INDEX - Continued

CANDLE BURNING MAGIC

By Anna Riva

ITEM #74748
$6.95

Everything you need to know to begin a candle ritual is included in this book. Learn the basic rules of candle burning, the different types of candles, how to create an altar, preparing and dressing candles, 125 candle rituals, prayer to the Saints and much more!

96 Pages

SPELLS to see the future • SPELLS to obtain great power •SPELLS to reunite estranged lovers • SPELLS to remove the need for drugs • SPELLS to bewitch others • SPELLS to learn secrets through dreams • SPELLS to break a hex or curse • SPELLS to attract love, luck, power & money • SPELLS to bind others to you • SPELLS to keep a lover faithful • SPELLS to contact departed souls • SPELLS to become fortunate in all matters • SPELLS to receive answers to prayers • SPELLS to solve problems • SPELLS to break up love affairs

www.wisdomproducts.com

INTERNATIONAL IMPORTS
PUBLISHER & DISTRIBUTOR OF NEW AGE BOOKS

BOOKS IN PRINT

- ❑ 70372 Black & White Magic - by Marie Laveau $5.95
- ❑ 74748 Candle Burning Magic - by Anna Riva $6.95
- ❑ 70344 Crystal Gazing 6 lessons Revised - by Dr. Ra Mayne $2.95
- ❑ 74751 Devotion to the Saints - by Anna Riva....................$6.95
- ❑ 79969 Domination - by Anna Riva....................$5.95
- ❑ 77012 Golden Secrets of Mystic Oils - by Anna Riva....................$7.95
- ❑ 70007 Guiding Light - by Mikhail Strabo $5.95
- ❑ 75969 How to Conduct a Seance - Revised by Anna Riva $2.95
- ❑ 77883 How to Use a Ouija Board - Michael St. Christopher........$5.95
- ❑ 77726 King Tut Dream Book $6.95
- ❑ 73952 Magic with Incense & Powders - by Anna Riva $6.95
- ❑ 72100 Modern Herbal Spell Book - by Anna Riva....................$5.95
- ❑ 70291 Modern Witchcraft Spell Book - Anna Riva $5.95
- ❑ 73954 Old Love Charms & Spells - Michael St. Christopher $5.95
- ❑ 76777 Powers of the Psalms - Anna Riva....................$6.95
- ❑ 75299 Prayer Book - by Anna Riva $6.95
- ❑ 72260 Prayers to the Saints....................$4.95
- ❑ 72293 Secrets of Magical Seals - by Anna Riva $5.95
- ❑ 72253 Spellcraft, Hexcraft & Witchcraft - by Anna Riva $5.95
- ❑ 73987 Spiritual Cleansing - Draja Michaharic....................$7.95
- ❑ 70100 Voodoo Handbook of Cult Secrets - by Anna Riva...........$5.95
- ❑ 76602 Witch's Spellcraft Revised - by Tarostar $6.95
- ❑ 77480 Your Lucky Number Forever - by Anna Riva $7.95

Ask for these books at a bookstore, spiritual supply store or botanica. You can also order from us. Check the boxes next to the books you have selected. Add the total. Shipping costs are $2.50 for the first book and 75¢ for each additional book. California residents add 8.25% for sales tax. Sorry no C.O.D.'S. Canada and Mexico customers shipping costs $5.00 for the first title and $1.00 for each additional book. Foreign customers shipping costs $7.00 for the first title and $1.00 for each additional book.

SEND ORDER TO: WISDOM PRODUCTS
2750 S. Alameda St.
Los Angeles, CA 90058

Prices Expire Jan 2010

NAME: ____________________

Address: ____________________

City: __________ State: __________ Zip: __________

www.wisdomproducts.com